THE
WINDSOR
REPORT:
A LIBERAL RESPONSE

D1495013

THE WINDSOR REPORT:

A LIBERAL RESPONSE

Editors:
Jonathan Clatworthy and
David Bruce Taylor

BOOKS

Winchester, UK
New York, USA

Copyright © 2005 O Books
O Books is an imprint of John Hunt Publishing Ltd., Deershot Lodge,
Park Lane, Ropley, Hants, SO24 0BE, UK
office@johnhunt-publishing.com
www.O-books.net

Distribution in:
UK
Orca Book Services
orders@orcabookservices.co.uk
Tel: 01202 665432 Fax: 01202 666219 Int. code (44)

USA and Canada
NBN
custserv@nbnbooks.com
Tel: 1 800 462 6420 Fax: 1 800 338 4550

Australia
Brumby Books
sales@brumbybooks.com
Tel: 61 3 9761 5535 Fax: 61 3 9761 7095

New Zealand
Peaceful Living
books@peaceful-living.co.nz
Tel: 64 7 57 18105 Fax: 64 7 57 18513

Singapore
STP
davidbuckland@tlp.com.sg
Tel: 65 6276 Fax: 65 6276 7119

South Africa
Alternative Books
altbook@global.co.za
Tel: 27 011 792 7730 Fax: 27 011 972 7787

Text: © The Contributors 2005

Design: Jim Weaver Design
Cover design: Krave Ltd., London

ISBN 1 905047 29 0

A CIP catalogue record for this book is available from the British
Library.

Spelling is American throughout.

Printed in the UK by Ashford Press

CONTENTS

The Modern Churchpeople's Union

The Modern Churchpeople's Union is a forum for Christian debate and discussion which welcomes new insights in religious faith. It believes divine revelation has not come to an end. God invites us to do our believing in ways appropriate to the 21st Century. It therefore promotes open, honest searching for truth in a spirit of humility and respect.

The main regular event is an annual conference. There are also regional branches, and members are offered discounts on a variety of publications.

Membership enquiries and applications should be sent to Mr Alan Sheard, 7 Northfield, Swanland, North Ferriby, East Yorks, HU14 3RG, UK, Tel (home): 01482 633 971, Email: gilalsrd@fish.co.uk.

For all other correspondence with the MCU please consult the www.modchurchunion.org or contact the General Secretary, The Revd J Clatworthy, 9 Westward View, Aigburth, Liverpool, L17 7EE, UK, Tel 0845 345 1909 or +44(0) 151 726 9730, Email: office@modchurchunion.org.

FOREWORD

John Shelby Spong

The commission set up by the Archbishop of Canterbury, Rowan Williams, to determine how the Anglican Communion can maintain its unity while recognizing wide diversity of opinion about homosexuality has, with great fanfare, released its report. It is long, convoluted and about what one would expect from a frightened leadership that thinks that the problem is one of maintaining unity rather than seeking to discern the truth. Those who called for this study do not appear to understand that a church unified in ignorant devotion to its continuing homophobia is hardly a church worthy of much attention by anyone. This report is, therefore, nothing more than a pathetic ecclesiastical attempt at damage control. It will fail in its stated purpose today. It will, I fear, be nothing but an enormous source of embarrassment in the future.

The deficiency in this report begins in its inability to distinguish between the problem and the symptoms. The crisis confronting our church was not caused either by the ordination of the Rt. Rev. Gene Robinson, an openly gay man, to be the Episcopal Bishop of New Hampshire, or by the authorization in the Anglican Church of Canada of blessings for same sex unions. The real damage needing to be addressed was the blatant prejudice and hostility toward homosexual persons that occurred at the Lambeth Conference of the world's Anglican bishops in 1998. This once every ten years event, convened at the invitation of the Archbishop of Canterbury, was overwhelmed by a homophobic combination of First World Anglican evangelicals with Third World Bible-quoting Anglican fundamentalists, both being orchestrated by the inept leadership of the then Archbishop of Canterbury, George Carey. That particular alliance possessed more zeal than wisdom. The ensuing debate at that gathering reached a level of rudeness that I have never witnessed before in church circles. It was punctuated by hisses and catcalls made when those, who opposed the prejudice present in that gathering, tried to speak. George Carey violated every protocol. He sat on the stage in full view of his supporters gleefully leading the vote with his raised hand, as the amendments grew more and more severe. He then went to a microphone to say how pleased he was "that scripture had been upheld" in the vote, only to be reminded that the vote had not yet been taken! This was the first time in the three of these conferences I attended where bishops were actively lobbied in an effort fueled with American dollars, primarily from Texas. The progressive voices of the Church were so battered by their conservative opponents that for all practical purposes they withdrew from the fight. This conference ripped apart a report adopted with much struggle and compromise in its section assigned to deal with issues of homosexuality. That section had worked out a tenuous consensus with which no one was satisfied, but all sides were on board, only to see its work gutted in the plenary sessions by a series of hostile amendments, until the final resolution was overtly hostile, mean-spirited and deeply divisive. It was a Conference in which none of the persons who had both the office and the ability to offer effective leadership said a word. That included the primates of the United States, Frank Griswold and of Canada, Michael Peers, as well as the leading Welsh bishop, Rowan Williams, who even then was being talked about as the next Archbishop of Canterbury. He chose to play it safe. That should have been a tip-off to those who supported him, as to what sort of Archbishop he would be.

When the voice of one of these recognized leaders might have made a difference they were strangely silent. Others like the Archbishop of Capetown, Njongokullu Ndungane and the Primus of Scotland, Richard Holloway tried to fill that vacuum, but were shouted down. Finally, it was a Conference in which the majority of the world's Anglican bishops spoke about the Bible in a way that indicated an unawareness of the biblical scholarship that has emerged in Germany, the U.K. and the United States over the last two hundred years.

Archbishop Carey, in a perfect example of the 'Peter Principle,' sought to impose his narrow evangelical worldview on the whole Communion, not seeming to recognize that this international church is made up of wide cultural diversity. Some branches of the Anglican Communion, for example, live in cultures where women occupy top positions in law, politics, business and education; while other branches of this worldwide communion live in nations that practice polygamy and female circumcision, and where education is not provided for female children. No church anywhere can survive an attempted imposition of cultural uniformity on so wide a gap. Attitudes toward homosexuality run a similar gamut. In the United States gay males from both political parties are elected to the Congress and serve as ambassadors; in parts of Africa and Southeast Asia an openly homosexual person runs the risk of being murdered.

At an earlier Lambeth Conference in 1988 the issue of women bishops threatened to tear this Communion apart, but the skillful leadership of the then Archbishop of Canterbury, Robert Runcie, steered the bishops through these choppy seas with a grace that was transforming. Runcie, who did not himself support the ordination of women, nonetheless lived in a very large world and knew how to use the power of his office to help the Communion live creatively inside the inevitable tensions of an idea that could not be stopped.

George Carey had an opportunity to emulate that example, but his narrow evangelical mind wanted a vote to affirm his own negativity about homosexuality. He got it, but that vote was a hollow victory and its bigotry made our present divisions inevitable. He did not understand that rising consciousness can never be deterred by majority vote. Furthermore, he wanted every province of the Communion to agree not to pursue any steps aimed at including homosexual people in the full life of the church until a worldwide consensus had formed, and all provinces could move together. It was a familiar delaying tactic and an impossible demand. Anglicanism's most backward dioceses, whether in Sydney or Chad, can never bind the consensus on this subject now growing in Western countries. Only one who imagines that he or she alone possesses the truth of God could have thought that a proper tactic. That is the fatal evangelical flaw.

This Commission decided mistakenly that they were dealing with an issue of disunity, when they were in fact dealing with the evil of prejudice. That was clear when their solution was to invite those churches that have banished their homophobic prejudices to consider apologizing to those parts of the church that were offended by their inclusiveness. That would be like asking those nations that have thrown off the evil of segregation to apologize for hurting the consciences of the segregationists. It was an inconceivable request. Whenever growth occurs there is always conflict and dislocation. The world would still be practicing slavery, child labor and second class status for women, had not a new consciousness confronted our prejudices in a movement that always destroys the unity of the old consensus.

In an effort to appear evenhanded, this report also sought to speak a critical word to those Third World bishops now seeking to destabilize Anglican Church life in countries open to gay and lesbian people. This was also a meaningless gesture, since the very nature of the Anglican Communion affirms the independence of each national body. This means that this Commission has no power to order anything and, because of this, no one will pay much attention to it anyway.

Finally this Commission in an attempt to force this Communion into a sense of unity, called upon the thirty eight national branches of the Anglican Communion to sign a covenant expressing their support for something called, 'current Anglican teaching.' That remarkable request was surely designed to bring gales of laughter to anyone familiar with Anglican history! In a Church that has never recognized an infallible pope or an inerrant Bible, where is current Anglican teaching enshrined? Is it in the resolutions of the Lambeth Conference that has no authority, and in which only bishops vote? Would those Anglicans who have engaged critical biblical scholarship be asked to subscribe to the pre-modern mindset of some third world countries that oppose evolution, interpret the Virgin Birth as literal biology, or view the Resurrection as a physical resuscitation? Would we destroy the tradition of the great Anglican scholars of the past, and try to place 21st century minds once again into the pre-modern straitjacket of the Thirty Nine Articles of Religion that formed the Elizabethan Settlement? Would we institute an Anglican version of the Inquisition in order to restrain our scholars? Would we want to become a Church that no longer produced Ian Ramsey, William Temple, John Elbridge Hines, James Pike or John A.T. Robinson? These ideas are too ludicrous to contemplate. Robin Eames, the Anglican Primate of Ireland who chaired this Commission, knows these facts better than most. Yet this idea was included, which means this report was never intended to be more than a public confession that its purpose was not to address the crisis but to use rhetoric as a smokescreen to soothe hurt feelings. As such the report is a dishonest effort to achieve cheap unity by sacrificing reality and truth.

The Anglican Communion had a relatively minor crisis as it watched a new consciousness about homosexuality struggling to be born in the face of ancient ignorance and prejudice. This Commission, and the leadership that requested its formation, has turned this minor crisis into a full scale disaster that if heeded will move Anglicanism toward the literal-mindedness that now threatens not just Christianity, but religious systems all over the world. Death comes in many forms. The inability to embrace new reality is one of them.

Reprinted with permission from Waterfront Media, Bishop Spong's online publisher.

John Shelby Spong was the Episcopal Bishop of Newark, NJ, for more than twenty years, and is a leading spokesperson for progressive Christianity.

INTRODUCTION

B y the end of 2002 it was clear that the Anglican Communion was heading for a major internal dispute, and that the focal issue was the ethics of homosexuality. An event had taken place, which, while acceptable to many Anglicans, was unacceptable to others. A campaign of opposition emerged, unexpected by most Anglicans but so well organized that it soon became clear that it had been many years in the preparation.

The controversial event? The announcement that Rowan Williams, Archbishop of Wales, was to be the next Archbishop of Canterbury. Whatever his strengths or weaknesses, it was as though the only thing that matters about Archbishops of Canterbury is their views on homosexuality. Repeated, and heavily publicized, demands were made that he should not be permitted to take up his post. By the time of his enthronement, in February 2003, it was clear what we were in for.

Three months later a succession of events highlighted the disagreements over the issue. Jeffrey John, Chancellor and

Canon Theologian of Southwark Cathedral, was named the new Suffragan Bishop of Reading in the Diocese of Oxford. Canon John was living with another man, in a relationship which, he said, had previously been sexually active, and refused to repent of the practice. Again there was a well-organized high-profile campaign to get his appointment overturned. Philip Giddings, a leading figure in Oxford Diocese, threatened that parishes would refuse to pay their contributions to the common funds. *The Times* published a strongly worded letter by nine diocesan bishops, criticizing the appointment. Peter Akinola, the Archbishop of Nigeria, threatened to precipitate a schism if the appointment went ahead. Another open letter, signed by eight diocesan bishops, supported the appointment. Meanwhile the Diocese of New Westminster, in Canada, authorized a liturgy for blessing homosexual relationships, and Gene Robinson, who openly admitted to being in a gay relationship, was elected Bishop of New Hampshire in the USA.

At the beginning of July Jeffrey John formally asked for his nomination to be withdrawn. Pressure had been put on him by the Archbishop of Canterbury, who in turn had been pressurized by opponents of the appointment. From this point on the focus of the campaign was on Gene Robinson's appointment. Opponents had two significant threats at their disposal: to split the church, and to withhold their financial contributions to the central funds. The world outside church politics looked on with bemusement, wondering what sort of Christianity this was.

The Primates met in October to discuss the situation, and published a statement that blamed the Canadian rite for same-sex blessings and the election of Gene Robinson for threatening the Communion's unity. If Robinson's consecration were to take place, they said, "We have reached a crucial and critical point in the life of the Anglican Communion." They called on the

2

offending provinces "to make adequate provision for episcopal oversight of dissenting minorities". At its request the Archbishop of Canterbury set up a commission, chaired by Robin Eames, Archbishop of Armagh, to examine the theological and legal implications and make recommendations.

There was no shortage of previous documents to work on, taking a variety of positions. The *Osborne Report* (1989) had not been published because it was considered too liberal; *Issues in Human Sexuality* (1991) had been. This was a statement by the Church of England's House of Bishops that argued that the conscientious decision of those who enter homosexual relationships must be respected, with the exception of clergy, who may not do so because of "the distinctive nature of their calling, status and consecration". In 1997 the General Synod encouraged parishes to use it as a discussion document, while admitting that "it is not the last word on the subject".

At the Lambeth Conference of 1998 a resolution was passed which condemned homosexuality as "incompatible with scripture" and refused to advise "the legitimizing or blessing of same sex unions" or "ordaining those involved in same sex unions". At the same time it stated that the bishops committed themselves "to listen to the experience of homosexual persons". In 1993 the Church of England's House of Bishops had published a discussion document, *Some Issues in Human Sexuality*, which took a similar line.

The Commission was given a year to produce their Report. During this time the debate continued. Before Robinson's consecration various reactions like "impaired communion" were threatened if it went ahead. After his consecration demands shifted to some kind of "disciplining" of ECUSA, the Anglican Church in the USA. A key demand was that anti-Robinson parishes who had pro-Robinson bishops should be given the power to seek "alternative episcopal oversight". Many preferred to call it "adequate episcopal oversight".

The Commission invited submissions. It was inundated with opposition to New Westminster and New Hampshire. Among the contributions, a statement signed by fourteen primates declared that, "the recent action of the Bishop of New Westminster displays a flagrant disregard for the remainder of the Anglican Communion". The bishop had, apparently, "placed himself and his diocese in an automatic state of impaired communion with the majority". The Church of England Evangelical Council complained of "provocation by a liberal and revisionist elite on an orthodox and unsuspecting Church", a matter of the highest importance because "in classic Christian teaching, homosexual actions leave the actors facing God's judgment without Christ's mediating work ... both heaven and hell are genuine alternative destinies". Anglican Mainstream proposed that the bishops who attended Gene Robinson's consecration should no longer have their ministries recognized. The Statement of the Primates of the Global South declared that "in addition to violating the clear and consistent teaching of the Bible, the consecration [of Gene Robinson] directly challenges the common teaching, common practice and common witness within the one Anglican Communion", and urged the Archbishop of Canterbury to establish "adequate provision of episcopal oversight" urgently. "Drawing the Line", a submission by a group of bishops and theologians, argued for "restorative discipline", on the ground that "if there is to be no accepted discipline within the Communion, then there must be appropriate distance from the Communion". There were also submissions in support of same-sex blessings and the consecration of Gene Robinson; the following chapters will illustrate the nature of their arguments.

In January 2004 a secret letter was leaked to the press. Written by Geoff Chapman on behalf of the American Anglican Council, it explained that while, in public, they were asking for "adequate episcopal oversight", the real aim, being secretly planned on both sides of the Atlantic, was a major realignment of Anglicanism, a "replacement jurisdiction" to exclude the liberals. There followed four pages of detailed plans, describing a two-stage program. Stage 1 would consist of "spiritual realignment" while keeping "'within the letter of current canons". Parishes should announce that their relationship with their bishop is "severely damaged". In the meantime a network of supportive parishes would be built up. In Stage 2 the new system would be announced and negotiations begin in earnest regarding "property, jurisdiction, pastoral succession and communion". Ominously it continues, "If adequate settlements are not within reach, a faithful disobedience of canon law on a widespread basis may be necessary". The confidentiality of the document is stressed: recipients are told to share it "in hard copy (printed format) only with people you fully trust, and do not pass it on electronically to anyone under any circumstances".

As the date for publication of the Commission's report drew near, the debate was enlivened by leaks. On 2nd September, Ruth Gledhill wrote in *The Times* that it would recommend excluding ECUSA from the Anglican Communion, and only allow it back in when Gene Robinson retired, or was excluded from his post, provided that no more gay bishops were consecrated and no blessings of gay unions sanctioned. The following day Jonathan Petre told *Daily Telegraph* readers a milder story. Bishops who publicly support the consecration of Gene Robinson, or authorize gay marriages, would no longer be invited by the Archbishop of Canterbury to Anglican summits, and might yet be ejected in 2008, the date of the next Lambeth Conference, if they have not recanted before then.

When the Report was published, it came as a relief to liberals that the recommendations were not as severe as the leaks. Nevertheless it did not say what they would have liked to hear. It was not within its terms of reference to discuss the ethics of homosexuality, but it made it clear where it stood:

> The Communion has... made its collective position clear on the issue of ordaining those who are involved in same gender unions; and this has been reiterated by the primates through their endorsement of the 1998 Lambeth Conference resolution [which condemned homosexuality]. By electing and confirming such a candidate in the face of the concerns expressed by the wider Communion, the Episcopal Church (USA) has caused deep offence to many faithful Anglican Christians both in its own Church and in other parts of the Communion (127).

Opposition to Gene Robinson's consecration, it declares, is the overwhelming response of other Christians (28).

The Report emphasizes the importance of unity, and discusses the role of Anglicanism's "instruments of unity": the Archbishop of Canterbury, the Lambeth Conference, the Anglican Consultative Council and the Primates' Meeting. "Provincial autonomy", it declares, "was framed by Anglican inter-dependence on matters of deep theological concern to the whole Communion" (21).

But are gay bishops a matter of deep theological concern, or are they *adiaphora*, an issue on which different positions may be taken? The Report accepts that Christian doctrines do not have to stay the same for all time; theology can, and does, develop. Agreed methods for making judgments are therefore needed (32). New developments have been subjected to a process of reception; that is, they are tested by how the faithful receive them. It describes the process in three stages: theological debate, formal action, and increased consultation (68). However, it continues that

> The doctrine of reception only makes sense if the proposals concern matters on which the Church has not so far made up its mind. It cannot be applied in the case of actions, which are explicitly against the current teaching of the Anglican Communion as a whole, and/or of individual provinces. No province, diocese or parish has the right to introduce a novelty, which goes against such teaching, and excuse it on the grounds that it has simply been put forward for reception (69).

In other words, the Report denies that same sex blessings and the consecration of a gay priest as bishop are legitimate examples of the process of reception: these events, it believes, should not have taken place without a much wider consensus of the worldwide Communion.

How, then, do we decide which issues count as *adiaphora*? The Report offers two criteria. Firstly, is it "the kind of matter which can count as 'inessential', or does it touch on something vital?" Secondly, is it something which "a sufficient number of other Christians will find scandalous and offensive, either in the sense that they will be led into acting against their own consciences or that they will be forced, for conscience's sake, to break fellowship with those who go ahead?"

The Report's specific recommendations are as follows. The Lambeth Conference and the Primates' Meeting both currently take place at the invitation of the Archbishop of Canterbury. This dependence on him should be enhanced:

The Archbishop of Canterbury should invite participants to the Lambeth Conference on restricted terms at his sole discretion if circumstances exist where full voting membership of the Conference is perceived to be an undesirable status, or would militate against the greater unity of the Communion (110).

There should be a "communion law" to strengthen the bonds of unity (117). There should be a "common Anglican Covenant" which would "make explicit and forceful the loyalty and bonds of affection which govern the relationships between the Churches of the Communion" (118). This is necessary because "the Anglican Communion cannot again afford, in every sense, the crippling prospect of repeated worldwide inter-Anglican conflict such as that engendered by the current crisis" (19).

Bishops are appointed locally, but as they have universal significance the appointment process should consider the acceptability of the appointment to other provinces (124, 131).

It recommended that "the Episcopal Church (USA) be invited to express its regret that the proper constraints of the bonds of affection were breached in the events surrounding the election and consecration of a bishop for the See of New Hampshire, and for the consequences which followed" (134). Such an expression of regret is a far cry from the repentance and discipline demanded by some. Nevertheless it implies that the controversy was caused by the Gene Robinson's election and consecration, not by his opponents, and expects them to agree.

It continues that "such an expression of regret would represent the desire of the Episcopal Church (USA) to remain within the Communion" (134). ECUSA's desire to remain in it is not, in fact, under doubt: the only members of ECUSA to suggest that it should leave are opponents of Robinson's consecration. The

Report's remark seems, therefore, best interpreted as a threat that its membership will be withdrawn if it does not so regret.

Pending such expression of regret, the Report continues, those involved in Robinson's consecration "should be invited to consider in all conscience whether they should withdraw themselves from representative functions in the Anglican Communion" (134). There is no proposal that they should be systematically excluded, but the path to such exclusion has already been indicated by the proposal that the Archbishop of Canterbury should feel free to withhold invitations.

A moratorium on the appointment of gay bishops is proposed "until some new consensus in the Anglican Communion emerges" (134). Thus the possibility of a new consensus, sympathetic to gays and lesbians, is accepted, though in practice it is rendered unlikely by the new proposals to demand Communion-wide consensus before making changes.

Many opponents of Robinson's consecration were disappointed that the Report did not take a sterner line. The contributors to this book are equally disappointed, but for different reasons. The wording of the rebukes is much milder than it might have been, and the actions proposed offer a gentler, more pastoral way to heal the wounds; but the blame is still placed squarely on those involved in the consecration, not on those who opposed it and threatened schism.

Colin Slee, as Dean of Southwark, was centrally involved in the controversy over Jeffrey John, who at the time was Canon of Southwark Cathedral. In his first contribution he notes that there is nothing new about controversy in the Church. He explodes the myth that homosexuality is universally condemned in the undeveloped world, and warns that the conservatives' threats to use their financial muscle should not be taken more seriously than they merit. In the second he discusses why the bishops have failed in their role of *episcope* (literally "oversight") by allowing this situation to develop, questions some of the practical proposals in the Report, and explores the issue of the search for purity in the Churches.

David Taylor challenges the Report's opposition to innovations made by bishops, and its proposal for a more centralized decision-making structure. The Report notes the pain caused to opponents of homosexuality, but not the greater pain caused to homosexuals themselves. Taylor accepts that the apostle Paul disapproved of homosexuality, but shows that evangelicals do not consistently accept the authority of the New Testament on ethical matters. He shows that the Report's proposals would make it impossible for changes to be made.

Gill Cooke questions whether bishops have, in practice, listened to the experience of homosexuals, as the 1998 Lambeth Conference resolution required, and proposes that the Church should take much more seriously the best and most recent evidence about sexuality from psychiatric research. She challenges the Report's discussion of the difference between essential and non-essential beliefs, and notes how many beliefs considered essential today – like opposition to racism and child abuse – were widely rejected by the church in the past.

Anthony Woollard compares the present debate with the Donatist controversy in the 4th century, where it was argued that "unworthy" ministers should be rejected. While recognizing the attractiveness of the idea that, when there is disagreement, everybody should wait for a consensus, he argues for a proper role for prophetic action. He discusses the problems we have regarding sexuality, where it appears as though humans have been created to behave in a way that does not match Christian spirituality. He explores the way natural law, and the role of experience, have been used in debates about sexuality.

Jonathan Clatworthy sets the current debate within the context of a wider disagreement. He notes the historical development of key beliefs about Scripture, tradition and reason, and how past circumstances have molded the doctrines of liberals and conservatives. The conservative tradition, with its over-confident claims to certainty and its suspicion of public research and debate, shows little patience with those who disagree with its views, and is all too willing to exclude them. The liberal tradition is much closer to the methods of truth-seeking used in other fields of discourse, and by taking a humbler, more democratic approach is better able to resolve disagreements.

This volume, prepared within a few weeks of the Report's publication, illustrates the characteristic responses to the Report by liberal Anglicans in the UK. The initiative for producing it came from the Modern Churchpeople's Union, of which all the authors except one are members. The role of the MCU is to promote liberal theology. The word "liberal" currently has a variety of different meanings; the type expressed here is a theological liberalism, of committed Christians who affirm a balance of Scripture, reason, tradition and experience and therefore believe that there is a proper role for change and development in our understanding of what is true and right. True, there are some biblical texts that condemn homosexuality. True, Christianity has condemned it for much of its history. But there are good reasons for questioning this condemnation, and the Church should have the humility to admit that it may have been wrong.

Jonathan Clatworthy

AN APPROACH TO
THE COMMISSION

This is an edited version of the representation that the
Very Revd Colin Slee, Dean of Southwark, made to the
Eames Commission. Only the argument is included; the
questions he directed to the Commission have been omitted.

I am addressing this to the Commission because I was at
the heart of the events of the summer of 2003 when my
colleague Canon Jeffrey John was put under pressure to resign
his acceptance of the nomination to the Bishopric of Reading. I
both witnessed and experienced the nature of that nomination
and resignation and believe that close experience places me in a
privileged position to make some observations that will, I hope,
be helpful to the Commission. I know the Commission has not
asked for evidence from Canon John, although I am aware it has
heard evidence from some who fiercely opposed his appointment.
I feel it would be worthwhile if the Commission asked him to
contribute as a matter of objectivity and balance, and a matter of
concern if it does not. He is, after all, an acknowledged theologian
and teacher.

Scripture has ample evidence of divisions between the
disciples in the New Testament. We would not have either the
epistles or the Revelation to St John the Divine if it had not been

for deep divisions within the early Church. The disciples are recorded as competitive and bickering in the gospels. It is plain that St Peter and St Paul represented polarized positions in the early Church. The New Testament only records them meeting three times and each time they had a row. Nevertheless, they also – and significantly – recognized the veracity and authentic discipleship of each other's views; they were "in Communion". The Reformation, the Enlightenment, the Free Church Movements, are all periods of challenging debate and upheaval within the Church.

The present debate has a very selective view of history within the Church. Many of the people on either side of the present debate would, in different circumstances, describe the old divisions of the Churches as sinful, a bad witness to the world, a source of shame; they will be people who regard ecumenical co-operation as a good thing to pursue. Nobody today would defend the religious persecutions and martyrdoms of the Reformation, or later disagreements when bishops were simply unfrocked because they acted according to their conscience. Nevertheless, many who express their horror at the conduct of our predecessors espouse a doctrinaire Anglican Church which, for example, demands public repentance (a feature of Reformation persecutions, and a demand laid against Canon Jeffrey John several times last summer), or engages in condemnation, and clearly discriminates against certain classes and types of people with regard to membership and status within the Church.

I spent two years working for the Anglican Church in Papua New Guinea (PNG). The Province of PNG is now numbered among those that have espoused a very traditional interpretation of Anglican teaching with regard to homosexuality. During my time there, I worked with a number of homosexual clergy, not all of whom were wholly celibate. I watched as all the Churches in PNG benefited from an agreement made between the World Wars, which divided the country into zones, so that denominations were no longer in competition but accepted responsibility for certain regions exclusively: the Comity of Churches. When boys from the school where I worked went to study in another region, we wrote to the pastor or priest commending them to their care, they were in communion on the basis of baptism and *vice versa*. The Province owes much to a mutual respect of central beliefs, baptism and acceptance of doctrinal difference within and between the Churches. It is a Province which, no matter what its present declared "policy" might be, was the beneficiary of the dedicated and fruitful ministry of priests whose sexual orientation was very different from that which is at present claimed as "orthodox". I believe that, almost by definition, because of the demands upon missionaries in the 18th, 19th and 20th centuries, this pattern may be applicable very widely.

For example, the penal colony at Sydney Cove, Australia, in the 18th and 19th centuries received many convicts from the Irish rebellion. It was very far from communication and regulation, and its chaplaincy was supplied by clergy who themselves had reason to wish to be away from England. There was therefore the mixture of tyranny and oppression with political hatred labelled by religious affiliation. Understanding the roots of the present intolerant Puritanism manifesting itself in a most un-Anglican way in the Sydney diocese (as recently discussed very widely in the media) requires recognition of Sydney's particularly unfortunate foundation and the effect of strong Irish connections. The conduct of the present Archbishop and his brother the Dean, may be giving cause for special concern within the Communion as being unrepresentative of the Anglican tradition to the point of being un-Anglican. It must be clearly recognized, nevertheless, that the present situation is the result of very many years of

Anglican sectarianism there. Archbishop Michael Ramsey denounced the bigotry of the Sydney diocese from the pulpit of Sydney's Anglican cathedral forty years ago.

I am in close contact with clergy, bishops and trainers as far apart as Brazil, Ethiopia, South Africa, New Zealand, Australia and Zimbabwe. In most of those countries the Church struggles to maintain the breadth of scholarship that is readily available in the northern hemisphere, because facilities, access to teachers, scholars and records, is so much more limited. The advent of the World Wide Web may in part be remedying this, provided there is adequate access to it. One feature of much that was said from the so-called "Global South" (which usually, it should be noted, ignores South Africa, New Zealand and Australia) is that any attempt at theological argument during the past year has been notable for a very limited theological perspective.

The Anglican Communion very properly needs to build structures for relationship, understanding and "democratic" synodical decision making. These need to be based upon sound foundations, rather than curious accidents of Provincial development and disproportionate influence that is unrepresentative of the entire Communion's make-up, or the responsibilities within each part of it. There is a strong case for abolishing the present Lambeth Conference as too expensive and altogether unrepresentative of the nature of the Communion as a whole. A smaller conference, a development of the Primates' Conference, limited to diocesan bishops (without spouses), would be a more effective tool for leadership, feeding in to regional provincial conferences ("mini-Lambeths") financed by and within each region.

I will give one further example. Policy statements have been made on behalf of the "African" Anglican Church that clearly do not reflect the position of the South African Province. The

Primate of South Africa has personally told me of meetings of African bishops to which he has not been invited. I recently spent three months in South Africa, while there I had a two-hour interview with the Bishop of False Bay (a suffragan bishop of Cape Town); he is openly gay, he lives a celibate life, he was consecrated by Desmond Tutu with clear statements of his sexual orientation at the time, and a clear majority in his election. He tells me he has received only one poisonous letter in the ten years he has been a suffragan bishop. That also indicates that those who say the Archbishop of Cape Town (and his predecessor) are out of step with African opinion and their pronouncements are wildly inaccurate.

The consecration of Bishop Mervyn Castle in 1994 created no furore in the Anglican Communion. It is hardly known in many parts of the Communion that he is openly homosexual and celibate. There are, of course (and always have been), other bishops who are homosexual but have not openly declared themselves to be so – I am aware of at least two who have been consecrated in Southwark Cathedral by the former Archbishop George Carey during my time as Dean.

Financial power has become a tool for coercion within the Communion. There are credible and repeated allegations of bribery of bishops to vote a certain way at the last Lambeth Conference. These have been mentioned several times in the press; it is notable that no denials have been issued and no actions have been taken against those making the allegations.

We have seen finance used as a lever in the debate about the ordination of women to the priesthood in the UK and elsewhere, with people and parishes threatening to withdraw their giving. In the Diocese of Southwark, it was used when the Cathedral hosted a service for the Lesbian and Gay Christian Movement, six parishes refused to pay their quota, exerting a pressure on the diocese but none at all on the Cathedral; this was widely publicised at the time. What was not publicised was their confidential payment of their quota some months later. The parishes used financial withdrawal as a leverage device whilst benefiting from diocesan structures and then submitted to those structures in order to avoid any disciplinary measures.

Conservative evangelical groups have propagated the notion that they carry serious financial power and could cripple the Church by exercising that power. This argument has been clearly utilized within England, in the USA and Canada. It is a flawed argument theologically: Churches are in communion; they cannot be partly in communion on conditions. It is also fiscally doubtful that the case would stand up to true financial analysis. A snapshot of the largest donor parishes in this diocese to the diocesan share revealed, to some people's surprise, they were equally balanced between evangelical and catholic parishes.

If finance is to be accepted within the Communion as a legitimate bargaining tool, then the weight of authority clearly lies with those Churches that contribute most to the Communion. This is not an argument I would advocate but the figures speak for themselves. The Anglican Consultative Council publishes accounts showing that over four years the Church of England has given £1,357,731, the USA. £1,314,378, whereas Nigeria only £70,148, the West Indies £48,268, Australia £431,807 and Papua New Guinea £5,128. (This is in addition to Mission giving from the UK and USA Churches.)

The direction of the misuse of finance as a weapon for debate has been from conservative "evangelical" groups within the Communion against the wider, central and liberal "catholic" parts of the Communion. This is deeply unscriptural, despite the frequently declared loyalty of those parts of the communion to Scripture. There is an excellent paper and exegesis of this policy by the Bishop of Thetford, David Atkinson, published in the Diocese of Norwich last summer. It is a notable ecclesiological distinction that the "threat" to use financial leverage has almost never been employed in the opposite direction within the Communion against conservative and evangelical Provinces or parishes. Within the Church in the UK, wealthy evangelical congregations are nearly always suburban. Withdrawal of financial support is at the expense of the maintenance of the ministry of inner urban or rural, deprived parishes. This raises significant questions about the teaching of ecclesiology and exegesis in the prosperous parishes.

It is my personal opinion that there are Provinces and organizations within the Anglican Church dedicated to accepting anything they choose to like, while rejecting and subverting anything they dislike; there is a breakdown of discipline and an erosion of "Communion". There is clear evidence of this from the debate concerning the ordination of women to the priesthood. In the UK, the strategy for a divided Church was actually institutionalized by the Act of Synod. Those who chose to reject the validity of women's orders were given the privileged position of remaining within the Church (and in many cases continuing to subvert it), whilst rejecting its carefully debated path. These people and parishes are from *both* catholic and evangelical traditions. In New Zealand, the Church established the first "flying bishops" with the establishment of the separate Maori constituency and episcopacy. This action not only acted as a precedent for the Act of Synod in England (which, it may be argued, institutionalised dissent) but may also be open to question as a racist action, when its motives were no doubt the exact opposite.

There were many Anglicans, both in the UK and throughout the Communion, who do not represent the evangelical perspective he epitomised, who found Archbishop George Carey's appointment difficult to accept for several reasons; but they were loyal, there were no stratagems to undermine him or campaigns against his appointment, or organizations financed and dedicated to subvert his teaching.

It became abundantly clear to me during the course of the highly sophisticated campaign against Canon Jeffrey John during the summer of 2003 that there are organized networks dedicated to subverting the due processes of the Communion.

One example is the network that now emanates from the Oxford Centre for Mission Studies, based at Wycliffe College Oxford; another is Anglican Mainstream. The mobilisation of e-mail campaigns, letter writing and telephoning were, in organizational terms, impressive. The objective was the reversal of a decision properly taken within the open and public structures of a given Province, with the Archbishop's consent and the approval of the Crown; more openly and consultatively than in the appointment of any other suffragan bishop (of which I am aware) in the UK. An individual was pilloried by mass communication generated from a relatively small but highly organised group; the Archbishop was effectively subverted, the statistics, when assessed dispassionately, bear this out, because the numbers of communicant Anglicans who were not threatening actions to force Canon John's resignation enormously outweighed the numbers that were. It is a known statistical phenomenon that people write objections much more than they write approvals, the case for submitting to the campaigns from objectors is therefore always extremely doubtful on moral grounds. Overseas archbishops and bishops were recruited (by what mechanism?) to interfere in the proper processes of an independent Province, thereby creating the crisis the Commission must now address.

In debates concerning women's ordination, lay presidency,

divorce and homosexuality, there has been evidence that some parts of the Communion place emphasis on Scripture at the expense of Reason and Tradition, while others appeal to reason and could be said to give inadequate attention to Scripture. Reason is not only an intellectual tool in discerning meaning and doctrine but also in responding to the climate and social demands of the present era. These will differ from country to country. It is perfectly possible to hold the Communion together if the Communion can discern these three elements of its inheritance as in a constant dynamic dialogue, by which each enriches the other, and in different proportion in different parts of the world, and at different times.

Scriptural exegesis lies at the heart of many of the most divisive debates. One of the most distressing features has been the way that people who claim to teach the Scriptures seriously are hugely selective in the manner they use Scripture. For example: Our Lord had direct and firm things to say in the gospels about divorce but nothing about homosexuality. It is normally accepted that the gospels have a certain scriptural pre-eminence as a source. Yet the present Bishop of Winchester argued in the General Synod of the Church of England for a more compassionate approach in the Church's discipline towards divorce, using Scripture and the spirit of reconciliation and forgiveness within Scripture as a whole, whilst at the same time he was participating in the campaign against homosexuals in the Church, objecting to Canon John's nomination to Reading, in a campaign that made highly selective use of passages in the epistles and was planned in secret, contrary to Holy Scripture.

In recent years, we have witnessed words being "kidnapped" for purposes that are not reflective of their true meaning. So we have movements and organizations which claim they are "traditional", "orthodox", "mainstream", "Reform", "Forward in Faith", and so on. It is a matter of misrepresentation. For example, the ecclesiological and doctrinal inheritance of the Anglican Church is both catholic and reformed. It is its unique gift to Christian history that its polity has been balanced in this way, and has permitted of inclusiveness for all people of goodwill with great generosity. Therefore to seek to label any organization narrowly "mainstream" when it does not represent these traditions, or narrowly "catholic" (which is an oxymoron), or "reform", is to seek to hijack the inheritance for a limiting purpose of exclusion.

The Commission has been delegated a role within the Communion, which may be said to be quasi-Episcopal. The ordinal for bishops in *Common Worship* says:

> "A bishop is called to lead in serving and caring for the people of God and to work with them in the oversight of the Church. As a chief pastor, he shares with his fellow bishops a special responsibility to maintain and further the unity of the Church, to uphold its discipline, and to guard its faith. He is to promote its mission throughout the world. It is his duty to watch over and pray for all those committed to his charge, and to teach and govern them after the example of the Apostles, speaking in the name of God and interpreting the gospel of Christ. He is to know his people and be known by them… He is to be merciful, but with firmness, and to minister discipline, but with mercy. He is to have a special care for the outcast and needy …'"

It is my firm conviction that the present discord within the Communion can be redeemed and turned to good purpose under God. I pray, nevertheless, that this is not done by postponing disagreement to another day and disguising it as diversity.

With respectful attention to the Ordinal, we seek from the Commission: leadership, service, care; furthering unity, guarding faith; mission, teaching and governance; merciful firmness and discipline; with a special care for the outcast and needy.

I look for clear guidance from the Commission for the Communion about its honesty, use of power and finance and for charity towards one another under God.

TO SEE OR NOT TO SEE: THE SEARCH FOR PURITY

Colin Slee

I am often given cause to reflect that Southwark Cathedral stands on the southern end of London Bridge: that is the end where the heads of executed prisoners were displayed on pikes until they rotted off. Thomas à Becket is reported as preaching in Southwark on the last occasion he fled from London; his murder at Canterbury turned a church that was already a place of pilgrimage into one of the great icons of Christian identity. Pilgrims travelling to his shrine passed through London, and must necessarily pass by the church of St Marie Overie; pilgrim badges are still dredged from the mud under London Bridge. Most famously, Chaucer's Canterbury pilgrims begin at the Tabard Inn in the Borough High Street. The tales they tell have bored, frightened, excited and delighted school children ever since they were written. Many of those pilgrims tell of escapades that present-day Christians, even the liberal sort, would regard as, at the very least, exhibiting less than whole-hearted faithful Christian discipleship.

Within the present retro-choir notable heretics, including bishops and prebends of St Paul's, were tried and condemned to be burned during the reign of Queen Mary. John Harvard, born and raised within the parish, returned from Emmanuel College Cambridge, sold his late parents' business and sailed to the New World where his puritan views would be acceptable; founding, by his legacy and his library, at the end of his very brief existence there, what is now the wealthiest university in the world. These are all stories of sin and redemption, and sometimes it is a matter of debate and particular viewpoint as to which is which.

Just over forty years ago John Robinson, with a stall in Southwark Cathedral, published his slim volume *Honest to God*, and unleashed a row in which he was denounced as a modern heretic by some, and acclaimed by others as the hope for the Church's progress in to the 20th century. It was not Robinson's greatest work: *that* lay in his scholarship in the New Testament. Perhaps it was slim because a bishop of the present-day Church does not have time to publish fat volumes of heresy worthy of a trial in the retro-choir. Bishops are tied to committees and to regulating the Church; only the very single-minded insist on adequate time for thinking, studying, writing and teaching; when they do, they are accused, openly and covertly, of neglecting their administration. It is said that modern western democracies only get the governments they deserve; perhaps the modern Church also gets the bishops it deserves. We have taken away the time and the role of *episcope* – the shepherd of the flock whose work is to see, and by seeing to safeguard and to lead where the flock has not been before. There can be no justification for complaining about our bishops; they are the product of the system over which the Church has more control than it has ever had, and they perform duties, which the Church, by synodical processes, has laid upon them. If they are largely grey managers, administrators, personnel directors and public relations officers, then it is for the Church to reconsider what it asks for, and the skills which are necessary to a more far-sighted, scholarly and adventurous *episcope*.

I was at a meeting recently at which the chairman said, "There are three sorts of people: forest people, tree people and leaf people." It is of the nature of *episcope* that the Church needs forest people – who can see the entire wood and are concerned for the whole people of God. What we have done is so to regulate their role that we are getting leaf people, whose daily diet of pre-determined administration keeps their eyes down.

The Windsor report holds within its covers several tensions. They have the potential to become a great gift to the Anglican Church – and, because they are difficult, they have the potential to fail spectacularly. If they fail, then people will say, "We tried, but it did not work." That may not be true. The very fact that the Commission was created at all is the result of not trying. The infamous resolution 1.10 of the Lambeth Conference 1998, about which many questions as to process and propriety remain unanswered, (and the Commission dodges them quite explicitly) did one sensible thing: it asked for debate and discussion. That did not happen, not real debate and discussion. There were conversations between like-minded people, but very little debate between differently minded people. What happened was that the "liberal" part of the Anglican Church worldwide acted true to form: it was liberal. It relaxed and allowed other people to carry on unchallenged, and was also not particularly keen to summon up the energy to be challenged itself. The "conservative" part of the Church was more politically alert; awakened by the controversies surrounding the ordination of women as priests, it built upon the experience and mobilized a sophisticated and highly organized world wide network of contacts, able to punch far in excess of its weight. After Lambeth 1998 the Anglican Church simply did not try to engage in debate; people returned to their laagers, and continued to eye one another with suspicion. That suspicion proved well founded – on both "sides" – when Canon Jeffrey John's nomination as Bishop of Reading was closely followed by Canon Gene Robinson's election as Bishop of New Hampshire and the authorisation of same-sex blessings in New Westminster diocese in Canada. Both "sides" behaved true to form.

It will take a much longer perspective, and the careful scrutiny of Church historians, to explain why the bishops of the Church did not see this coming. I refer not to the individual nominations and elections (the leaves), but the entire shaking of the forest. Why did nine diocesan bishops in the UK find it necessary to gather in secret, while actually at a meeting of the entire House of Bishops, to hatch a plot to publish a letter without their colleagues' knowledge? Was it fear? Do they have no concept of the oft-used phrase "brother-bishop"? Why was it that Desmond Tutu could consecrate a man who is quite open about his homosexual orientation as Bishop of False Bay in the diocese of Cape Town completely and totally openly, and yet, nine years later, the Anglican Church worldwide is mobilised by the mechanism of e-mail to oppose the nomination of a similarly celibate, scholarly and faithful priest as Bishop of Reading? Why can Bishop Mervyn Castle tell of the one and only poisonous letter he has received since his consecration, while Canon Jeffrey John was – literally – deluged with filth? Is it because Desmond Tutu's authority was considered unassailable, but ten years later the relatively new Archbishop of Canterbury was seen as an easy target for subversion, and the plot had been well prepared in the intervening years? Is it simply that the intervening years were the decade of evangelism that did not evangelize, and the

Church was feeling even more marginal and threatened? Is it that the intervening same decade was the period when personal computers became commonplace, and instant communication globally, by text messaging and e-mail, became a weapon of mobilization that ancient historic institutions like the Anglican Church find hard to appreciate? Each of these is a leaf question, or at most a tree question; none of them is a forest question. The historians will have to have their day when some space has elapsed for perspective, as well as accurate detail, to emerge. Central to them all must be the forest question. The bishops of the Church have *episcope*; what happened to it?

The Windsor report attempts to address this question by giving attention to the meaning of "'Communion", and the "Instruments of Unity"; that is, the mechanisms by which the Communion is governed, through which bishops exercise their role. Herein lies one of the major tensions within the report – and indeed, the report itself rightly appreciates it is a microcosm of a central tension within the Anglican Church. The tension lies between coherence and unity on the one hand, and diversity as a creative force on the other. It is an attempt to square a circle. The Anglican Church could move its organizational emphasis in the direction epitomized by the Roman Catholic system, a Curia and Magisterium. That is clearly very tempting: boundaries will be clearer, rules set, and unity enforced. The Commission however rejects this model, and rightly sees it as un-Anglican. If this was the way that Anglicans believe the Church should be governed, then they could very easily become Roman Catholics at any time they choose; there is a steady, but untrumpeted, flow of Roman Catholics becoming Anglicans to reinforce the view that a Curia may not necessarily be heaven on earth. (There are, of course, also, Anglicans becoming Roman Catholics precisely because they do want the clarity of the Roman Catholic system, which rather proves my point.) The Commission gives a lot of space throughout its pages to the richness of the inheritance of the Anglican Communion by the route of its diversity. Michael Ramsey forty years ago remarked that the diversity of the Anglican tradition was both its greatest virtue and its Achilles heel.

As Anglicans debate this Report, and I hope most sincerely that they will debate it, they will all find that the tensions affect them. "Evangelical" Anglicans, who are opposed, for example, to the ordination of homosexuals (the language becomes instantly very blurred, and one has to insist on knowing whether they mean practicing homosexuals or would permit celibate homosexuals, and whether "celibate" means always, or there must be some public repentance) will, on the face of it, incline towards a stronger discipline and governance. However when that discipline and governance also indicates that they will need to observe Canon Law with regard to liturgy, and perhaps even to clerical dress; when they realise it means the Bishop can ask his clergy to be at the Chrism mass on Maundy Thursday, and they have an obligation of obedience to their Bishop to be there; then the centralized order becomes less attractive.

The matter has been most glaringly apparent in the United Kingdom for many years in the matter of second marriages of divorced people. Any appeal to Scripture with regard to divorce is on shaky ground if there is any permissive intent; Our Lord had quite a lot to say about it, he is not permissive, indeed quite condemnatory. However there are many evangelical clergy, not least the most recent Archbishop of Canterbury, who have encountered divorce and second marriage within their own family and accommodated it with a good conscience, who nevertheless denounce homosexuality (about which Our Lord had nothing to say) on the basis of an appeal to Scripture. There were many Evangelical clergy disobeying the Church's declared policy and conducting second marriages long before it was permitted, even by a Nelson's eye. One is bound to observe that such behaviour is a matter of trying to have your cake and eat it. Either the Church moves towards a more accountable discipline in governance (which the Report portrays as a covenanted relationship between provinces) or it lives with the tensions of diversity, creative and contradictory though they may be.

If the argument then moves to being one of first-order and second-order Scriptures, then of course the liberals within the Church will be delighted, because they have argued that Scripture needs to be approached as a unique source of revelation, and that revelation continues through its pages as we interpret it for the present day. However the liberal view is very far from being truly "liberal" in the sense that anything goes. If that were to be the meaning of liberal, then the declared intentions of the Archbishop of Sydney to find a way to introduce lay-presidency at the Eucharist might be of no concern to them, whereas it is a matter of grave concern. So liberals *are* looking for Church order; they too are balanced on the horns of a very Anglican dilemma in this and other matters.

It is perfectly possible to understand why the Archbishop of Sydney can write in an English newspaper, shortly after the publication of the Windsor Report, indicating that he is unhappy with it because it will not work. He may have had the surprisingly novel experience of discovering that many liberals agree with him. It will not work if people are looking to its pages for a solution; it may work in that unique institution, the Anglican Communion, if it is seen as a process; but process and the theology of reception imply a willingness to change to accommodate differences, the nature of which one does not necessarily have to approve, and that willingness is open to question, not least in the declarations of the Archbishop of Sydney.

It is hardly in the open spirit of diversity and debate that Peter Akinola, the Archbishop of Lagos, writing a tirade after he had abruptly left London when the report was published, stated, "We have been filled with grief as we have witnessed the decline of the North American Church, that was once filled with missionary zeal and yet now seems determined to bury itself in a deadly embrace with the spirit of the age." ... "Thus they are hell-bent on destroying the fabric of our common life, and we are told to sit and wait" (Anglican Communion News Service 3902, 19 October 2004). By contrast, the presiding Bishop of the Episcopal Church of the United States wrote, "It is extremely important that it (the Report) be read carefully as a whole and viewed in its entirety, rather than being read selectively to buttress any particular perspectives." "... Unless we go beyond containment, and move to some deeper place of acknowledging and making room for the differences that will doubtless continue to be present in our Communion, we will do a disservice to our mission. A life of communion is not for the benefit of the Church, but for the sake of the world." (The Most Revd Frank Griswold, October 18th 2004.)

The report places considerable emphasis upon its recommendations with regard to "The Instruments of Unity". Two significant proposals are: the creation of covenant agreements between Provinces, whereby they all agree to consult in any fundamental changes to practice (the question of what is really fundamental is never explored in any detail); and the creation of a Council of Advice for the Archbishop of Canterbury as the senior Primate within the Communion.

One is bound to ask what the purpose of any written covenant can be in the ordering of a Church that is already the vessel for the New Covenant? If we are people of God by virtue of our baptism, and Anglicans by virtue of our membership, then we have no need of lesser covenants to hold us together; we need to work on, explore and realize the sacramental significance of the covenant of which we are already participants. There is a great temptation, which is evident in almost every single report, certainly from Church House, to dress up pragmatic and managerial issues with a theological preface. The Windsor report falls in to the same trap. The matter of governance of the 44 Provinces of the Communion is a practical and political issue, which can quite legitimately be addressed in that language; (after all, he says, falling in to the very same trap himself, Anglicans have a uniquely high regard for incarnation, and management of the Church is incarnational!). It is my own view that the covenant notion, while being a vehicle for a very good and wide-ranging discussion between the Provinces about what unites us and what differentiates us, is ultimately not a vehicle for any unity. That unity will be seized when we have a better appreciation of our baptism. The Council of Advice is another layer of consultation, another tool for governance, a new Committee for an already over-clericalized Archbishop to sit upon. The Commission report does not really ever address the better use of the layers of consultation that already exist for the Archbishop – most obviously the entertainingly entitled "Primates Conference". If these avenues of consultation are not working, then what is wrong with them? Should they not be replaced, rather than in some way duplicated? It is my understanding that the Primates' Conference makes regular and copious use of consultants, lay and ordained, who are not Primates (in the ecclesiastical sense); so additional layers of expensive committee work, with their self-justifying instincts, should be avoided.

I have had the pleasure of the company of the Reverend Professor David Fisher, from North Central College, Naperville, Illinois, in my congregation for the last few months. David wrote to me very helpfully several times. In one e-mail he said, "One of the besetting ills of any discipline is that practitioners are inclined to see all particular problems as matters to which their peculiar branch of inquiry should be applied. Thus philosophers turn human dilemmas into theoretical differences between ethical theories, while theologians turn political controversies into theological questions about nature and grace. While it is often useful to shift focus away from the heat of a controversy to considerations of theory, there is the danger that doing so will absolutize and harden diversity of opinion into difference and "otherness".

It has been said frequently that the issue at the heart of the entire debate addressed by the Windsor Report is the matter of method and approach to Scripture. There can be no doubt whatsoever that the place of Scripture within our tradition is central to our faith. The report acknowledges this with a lengthy section (53 –56) on *The Authority of Scripture,* followed immediately by a section (57 – 62) on *Scripture and Interpretation.* It was not within the Commission's remit to enter deeply into studies of the texts of the Old and New Testaments, exegetical issues, translation from the original language, secondary translations and so on. It is sufficient that the report rightly identifies this as one of the major battlefields of tension within the Anglican Communion, as was all too evident by the use of selected texts in the controversies which caused the Commission to be established. "We can no longer be content to drop random texts into arguments, imagining that the point is thereby proved" (61). The Commission very firmly warns that the term, "The Authority of Scripture", is itself ambiguous, and wrongly used as a weapon against contradiction.

It is however a tendency that we can see within the salvation history of humanity that Scripture chronicles, that I believe to be even more central than the issue of different interpretations. This is because the issue to which I suggest we must address more attention is one which directly affects our approach to the issue of Scripture, its authority and interpretation, itself: it is the search for purity. Put simply – and too starkly in the present context – the Windsor Report contains within its pages the tension that is as old as religious understanding and aspiration itself: the tension between good and evil, between adherence to the perceived Will of God and disobedience. The Commission was created because the Anglican Communion is divided. There are those who believe there is a purity of Anglican faith that can be shown, has a historic definition, and cannot be permitted to venture beyond certain boundaries – specifically the blessing of same-sex unions, or the ordination of homosexual people, especially as bishops; but in fact the splits are also evident elsewhere, in the matters of the ordination of women, of polygamy, of lay presidency and therefore of orders etc. On the other hand, there are those who believe that Anglican purity lies in a more opaque Church with fuzzy edges, inclusive of everyone of good will; Anglican purity is precisely a matter of tolerance and diversity (to be distinguished from impurity).

The administrative recommendations of the Report are inclined towards some concept of Anglican purity, usually discussed in terms of "identity" which, I suggest, is both the heart of the debate we should be having, and also its most deceptive and difficult issue. It is to this area of discussion that I would like to see the bishops of the Church direct their most attentive intelligence. I say this for two reasons: for the parochial (in the sense of Anglican) reason that I suggest this is the heart of all the fighting. And peace will not be discovered until this is exposed as a debate worth holding; more importantly, however, I say this because I believe that the search for purity lies at the bottom of most of the enormous conflicts of the world today. The search for purity is intrinsic to fundamentalism – religious, political and social. If the Anglican Church can honestly address the psychological imperatives of the demand for purity, and the political implications of the quest, then we can offer the world insights and wisdom that could enable reconciliation and justice in desperately damaged places and people.

I am indebted once again to my congregation: Professor Fisher referred me to the work of Paul Ricoeur, *The Symbolism of Evil* (Beacon Press 1967). Ricoeur argues for a sequential, cross-cultural development in symbols of evil: Stain, Defilement, Sin, Guilt. Fisher comments:

> At the most basic level of stain/defilement, there is a contrast between the experience of an external something as an impure thing that infects, on the one hand, and an internal dread that anticipates avenging wrath for having been defiled, on the other. Out of this primitive sense of personal, individual stain/defilement, sin develops as a way of understanding the continuing relationship between all persons and the sacred or holy. Finally, in guilt, the nature of our "fault" is neither the result of contact with something external (stain/defilement), nor of the demands of god or gods (sin) but of a fundamental flaw within our own will. Guilt, as it were, extends all the way down!

The Commission was established because some members of the Communion have a different definition of sin than others. Some, as we have seen in the words of the Archbishop of Nigeria, see sin as institutionalized in the Church as well as the individual. The motivating goal of the Commission is the avoidance of schism and sectarianism (which are, I suggest, very different), and the preservation of unity: division of the Church is seen as sinful, and by definition therefore impure. However, where the Commission runs into difficulty is that it also sees diversity and difference as motivating forces for change in the search after Truth and therefore "pure".

This is as old as the Scriptures themselves. In Genesis the story of the Flood is about purity and the preservation of the elect. We are told that Noah understood what it was all about, but there seems little evidence in the narrative that his children were fully subscribers. (Medieval Mystery plays have traditionally depicted Noah's wife as a bit of a battleaxe, for whom purity was more a matter of good housekeeping than the lusts of the flesh.) The stories of the patriarchs are littered with tales that concern purity, Jacob's discovery of Rachel, his cousin, being just one example; even her name means 'a pure ewe lamb, bright eyed and pretty'. At the Exodus there is concern about intermarriage and the defilement of the "pure" Hebrew line. The endless tales of the destruction of the indigenous tribes and inhabitants of Canaan, the Hittites, Perizzites, Hivites, and all the other "ites", are concerned not so much with conquest as with ethnic cleansing. In the great Babylonian exile at the heart of Hebrew Scripture it is intermarriage while enslaved that is the major concern. In the New Testament Our Lord is constantly being questioned about impurity, by disease, by ethnic origin (Samaritans, and Gentiles, and Romans), by disability (deaf, dumb, blind, demoniac), by occupation (tax collector, prostitute, Pharisee). Matthew begins his gospel narrative with a genealogy of Christ which contains four women, unusual in itself: they are there because each of them is impure. In the Epistles a war is raging between the Jerusalem Church that was reluctant to welcome the uncircumcised, and the Pauline missionary Church, which saw the Spirit of God descending even on those who had not yet been baptised.

These conflicts can be translated to the dilemmas of the Anglican Church in the 21st century. They are not new, just as the debates about welcoming servant classes, divorcees, and illegitimate children, or clergy with moustaches, have only recently been resolved. There is at the heart of all these debates, the great paradox of the redemptive love of God, namely that what we see in the present moment as a great divide can, in the perspective of history, seem extraordinarily trivial. The Church (since Noah!) has never been entirely pure, because God created men and women in his image – and that means, precisely, with free will and the capacity for sin. It is God therefore who created an impure Church, and the Church's problem is in accepting the will of God and welcoming the entire diversity of his creation.

If the Windsor report can help us to see, then we shall perhaps understand purity a little more clearly, and be less concerned to reach it by our own efforts.

The Very Revd Colin Slee is Dean of Southwark

DO AS I SAY, AND NOT...

David Bruce Taylor

There is a ghost haunting the Windsor Report, a shadowy figure of whose presence we are all aware, but must apparently pretend we haven't noticed. What shocks Archbishop Eames more than anything is that any Anglican bishop should presume to introduce innovations in his own (or I suppose we must now start talking about "their own" diocese), without reference to the susceptibilities of the wider Communion. Among the four "Instruments of Unity", on whose operation we must apparently rely if we are to prevent this happening, first and foremost (see page 55) is the Archbishop of Canterbury. Indeed, throughout Section C, and particularly in paragraphs 108-110, the position of the Archbishop is made out to be so pivotal for the restoration and preservation of the Anglican Communion that I suspect the man himself will be as embarrassed as the rest of us are likely to be surprised by it. The Anglican Communion portrayed in the Windsor Report is a very different kind of organization from the Church of England that I have been familiar with for more than fifty years now, nor am I by any means convinced of its superiority.

But to return to the ghost. If innovation is so to be regarded as a sin, what are we to make of the man who, in connection with Canon (as he then was) Jeffrey John, publicly agreed to his appointment as Bishop of Reading? That innovation, had it gone ahead, would have been far more daring than the consecration of Gene Robinson as Bishop of New Hampshire. True, the other American bishops approved his appointment and participated in the consecration, but none of them participated in the original appointment, which was by election by a large majority of the members of the diocese. (One of the difficulties the Windsor Report declines to tackle is: what are members of the hierarchy to do when the diocesan synod resoundingly and persistently votes for an innovation which they know will incite traditionalists to fury? Paragraph 137 of the Report makes it clear that Bishop Ingham resisted long and hard the demand of his synod for provision of a public Rite of Blessing for same-sex unions. The demand was made in 1998, and again in 2001; it was only at the third attempt in 2002 that he eventually gave way, and it is hard to see how he could have done otherwise, no matter what the reaction in the Communion at large might be.)

Rowan Williams' initial reaction to the suggested appointment of Jeffrey John as Bishop of Reading makes it perfectly clear that in his heart at any rate he lusted after innovation; and at least one notable authority assures us that is as bad as committing the actual offence. In this instance he walked right to the edge of Lovers' Leap, and it was only after looking in horror at the swirling waters below that his courage failed him, and he drew back and yielded to the embrace, which up to that time he had been anxious to avoid, of conservative evangelicals. But the Report carefully avoids any mention of all this, and expects us to clear our minds of the memory of it when we come to read its recommendations.

This is but one instance of its partiality, its hesitancy in criticizing those whose obduracy is the real cause of the division, its forthright condemnation of those who, in both instances, were essentially reacting to the demands of their fellow Christians in the locality; it is hard to see, in either case, how the reaction could have been anything other than it was. It has a lot to say about the pain these actions have caused conservative evangelicals; it has nothing to say about the infinitely greater pain, with infinitely less excuse, that those same conservatives have caused the homosexual community. They themselves appear to be perfectly aware of this pain, indeed to congratulate themselves upon it: as far as they are concerned, it is this very pain which proves to them they really are speaking to the world directly with the voice of God, and the plain evidence of Scripture is the absolute proof that this is so.

Let us take a look at these Scriptural claims of the opposition. They themselves are insistent upon them, and the Report never questions them; on the contrary, without unambiguously saying so, it tends to imply a full acceptance of them. The question falls into two halves: first whether Scripture really says what they say it does; and then whether we can really accept they sincerely believe what they say about its authority.

On the first point the argument is that no matter what we may privately feel about the predicament of homosexuals – that they might be right, for instance, in arguing that their condition is wholly the consequence of nature, that it is as necessary to them to express their feelings the way they do as is heterosexual love to heterosexuals, that since they have no real choice about this it cannot be made a question of morality – all this must be set aside for the simple reason that it is incompatible with what

Scripture has to say. There is a tradition among liberals, which I personally find unfortunate, that this is a misinterpretation of Scripture, and that its prohibition is not against homosexuality as such, but in reality against such plainly immoral conduct as male prostitution, or the fixation on the physical attractions of immature males. (It would be a mistake, by the way, to call them boys; it is clear from the literature that the ideal male sexual partner to the ancient world was the post-pubescent, but still largely pre-shave, youth.) But evangelicals are right to insist there is nothing in the New Testament which supports this distinction, where we find a condemnation of homosexuality that is not only unambiguous but also unambiguously comprehensive. Contrary to what some liberal scholars argue, we have no reason to believe that the idealized view of homosexuality as a noble, unselfish, elevating passion — that we find for instance in the works of Plato — was unknown to Paul, or at least not condemned by him; on the contrary, it is only too probable that Paul was enraged by this tradition even more than by the frankly lustful attitudes portrayed in such literature as, for instance, Martial's epigrams, where noble, unselfish, elevating passions of any kind are unknown, and would be dismissed as romantic foolery if they were encountered. The latter could be condemned as sin that was fully aware of its sinfulness and, because it was so aware, held out some hope of repentance; but the former was much more serious, in that it was sin masquerading as virtue, thus deliberately closing off the path to a new and better way of life. I fully accept the evangelical insistence that this is Paul's attitude in the New Testament.

So they have won the argument? In fact no. They are right about what Paul says; it is the claims they make for what he says that must be questioned. To admire the writings of Paul, to find any number of excellent precepts and perceptions in them — all that is fine; to go on to claim that Paul was in fact totally above criticism, was never mistaken in anything he said, to claim that if Paul said it, then it follows that God said it too – which is the necessary basis of the above argument – that is to stray from the path, not merely of truth, but of sense, of honesty and, in this case, also of charity.

But their claim to utterly faithful obedience to Scripture can be questioned on far more persuasive grounds. When one looks at their writings, though they frequently quote Scripture, it is always from only a very small section of it – from John's Gospel to the Apocalypse; in my Bible that is from page 1907 to 2155, about 11½ per cent of the whole. These days the almost complete omission of the Old Testament will seem shocking only to a few of us, but that of the Synoptic Gospels (Matthew, Mark and Luke) will seem remarkable to all; particularly in that, although none of the gospels can honestly be viewed as a worthwhile historical source for the life of Jesus, it is clear from details of the evidence of those first three gospels that he did actually exist, and that it is those three gospels only that contain such details. If we want to know anything at all about the actual life of Jesus, it is to those documents alone that we refer. John's Gospel tends to be praised as the most theological of the four, and this is justified; but the obverse of that praise is that it is also the least historical.

When we look at the Synoptic gospels, one noticeable feature of Jesus' teaching in them is his instruction about what it costs to be a disciple. The most striking examples are found in Luke's Gospel:

> "If anyone comes to me and does not hate his own father and mother and wife and children and brothers and sisters, yes, and even his own life, he cannot be my disciple."
> (Luke 14:26)

or:

> "So therefore, whoever of you does not renounce all that he
> has cannot be my disciple."
> (Luke 14:33)

but these are only the most extreme forms of a teaching which is
found in all three synoptic gospels, stated clearly, unambiguously,
repeatedly; there can be no doubt of its basis in historic fact.
Now those of us who are familiar with the lifestyle of evangelical
clergy will know that on the whole they live pretty well, and
that none of them has any intention of "renouncing all that he
has". On the contrary, they tend to have wives (which Jesus tells
them they should ditch), and children (likewise), and a house,
and a car, and an extensive wardrobe, and a good income, and
probably also an adequate pension; and I for one have no wish
to criticize them for any of these things, though there are plenty
in the world at large who do. But it is not merely hypocrisy but
gross and shameless impudence, having the material they have
before their eyes and happily ignoring all of it, to then turn
round to homosexuals and say, "We're sorry, but we have to give
you a hard time because Scripture says we must, and we have an
absolute obligation to obey Scripture." If they can be as selective
in their obedience to Scripture as they clearly are, they cannot
deny homosexuals, not even the homosexual clergy, the right
to exercise the same discretion – particularly when evangelicals
have freely chose to be evangelical, whereas homosexuals in the
main have not chosen to be homosexual.

Paragraph 39 of the Report reads:

> The [fourth] reason for our present problems is thus that it
> was assumed by the Episcopal Church (USA) and the Diocese
> of New Westminster that they were free to take decisions

on matters which many in the rest of the Communion believe can and should be decided only at the Communion-wide level.

This is to argue that changes can never be made, since it is hard to foresee the kind of universal consent that Dr Eames envisages being offered to any particular change. How does this square with what we find in the New Testament, following the conversion of Cornelius in Acts, chapter 10?

> Now the apostles and the brethren who were in Judea heard that the Gentiles also had received the word of God. So when Peter went up to Jerusalem, the circumcision party criticized him, saying, "Why did you go to uncircumcised men and eat with them?"
> (Acts 11:1-3)

The situation is exactly parallel to the one we are faced with now. The evidence is good that Jesus himself never envisaged a following that would have included Gentiles. "Go nowhere among the Gentiles, and enter no town of the Samaritans," (Matthew 10:5) would not of itself convince us were it not for the fact that we have the whole of Mark, chapter 7 to confirm it. The apparently pointless debate about ritual washing in the early part of the chapter (verses 1-23) ties in with the vision Peter is said to have seen of all sorts of animals, clean and unclean, being let down from heaven for him to eat. It is clear that "liberals" of the early Church were trying to get round Jesus' authentic prohibition against preaching to Gentiles by arguing that he had abolished the distinction between the clean and the unclean (which he does not in fact ever seem to have done). Also the change of heart he showed to the Syrophœnician woman in Mark

7:24-30 is clearly intended to prove that Jesus' rejection of the Gentiles was not as inflexible or dogmatic as Peter's opponents were insisting (which it does, while nevertheless confirming the fact of the rejection itself).

So Peter's critics appear to have been right to insist that his preaching had never been intended by Jesus for a non-Jewish audience. It is Peter's innovative act that falls heavily under Dr Eames' censure, while his critics are vindicated; fortunately for subsequent history, the early Church came to just the opposite conclusion. And when we read:

> When they [*Peter's critics*] heard this they were silenced. And they glorified God, saying, "Then to the Gentiles also God has granted repentance unto life".
> (Acts 11:18)

If we know anything at all either of human nature or Church history, we can be sure that this is a somewhat rosy account of how the issue was resolved. There were some, no doubt, who were convinced by Peter's narrative, and who were therefore silenced and induced to glorify God. But there was undoubtedly a considerable number who would have none of it, who therefore threatened (like their spiritual descendants today) that if the policy were not reversed, if Peter were not compelled to perform some public act of repentance, if no undertaking were given that no further conversions of Gentiles would be accepted, there would be firstly a withholding of contributions, and if that failed there would then be outright schism. And we need not doubt that some kind of schism did follow; but fortunately the future proved to lie with the innovators, as it has so often ever since.

The Christian Church has, right from the time of Paul, placed enormous emphasis on the need for unity, a theme, which is echoed throughout the Report, which opens with a consideration of the epistle to the Ephesians on this topic. I do not myself think that Ephesians is a genuine Pauline epistle, but that makes little difference to the argument, since there is plenty of undoubtedly genuine Pauline material to the same effect:

> I appeal to you, brethren, by the name of our Lord Jesus Christ, that all of you agree, and that there be no dissensions among you, but that you be united in the same mind and the same judgment. For it has been reported to me by Chloe's people that there is quarrelling among you, my brethren.
> (1 Corinthians 1:10-11)

or:

> So if there is any encouragement in Christ, any incentive of love, any participation of the Spirit, any affection and sympathy, complete my joy by being of the same mind, having the same love, being in full accord and of one mind.
> (Philippians 2:1-2)

Is this (to borrow a useful distinction made by the present Prime Minister) to be regarded as a definite policy, or merely as an aspiration? Let's test it against the known facts and see:

> And after some days Paul said to Barnabas, "Come, let us return and visit the brethren in every city where we proclaimed the word of the Lord, and see how they are." And Barnabas wanted to take with them John called Mark [*i.e. in Aramaic circles, where he really belonged, he was called John; to the Romans and Greeks, and the international community generally, he was Mark*]. But Paul thought best not to take with them

one who had withdrawn from them in Pamphylia, and had not gone with them to the work. And there arose a sharp contention, so that they separated from each other...
(Acts 15:36-39a)

or:

But when Cephas [*Peter*] came to Antioch I opposed him to his face, because he stood condemned. For before certain men came from James [*probably Jesus' brother, who seems to have presided over the Christian community in Jerusalem*], he ate with the Gentiles; but when they came he drew back and separated himself, fearing the circumcision party. And with him the rest of the Jews acted insincerely, so that even Barnabas was carried away by their insincerity.
(Galatians 2:11-13)

Clearly the thinking and practice of the Anglican Communion has a long previous history! In this case it is Peter and his fellow-hypocrites who are following the Eames doctrine, while Paul's principled stand is to be accused of tearing at the bonds of fellowship and unity. But apart from that, though Paul praises unity and fellowship in others, he demonstrates the limitations of that philosophy in his own practice.

The ideal of unity is exquisitely hymned in the New Testament:

I therefore, a prisoner for the Lord, beg you to lead a life worthy of the calling to which you have been called, with all lowliness and meekness, with patience, forbearing one another in love, eager to maintain the unity of the Spirit in the bond of peace. There is one body and one Spirit, just as you were called to the one hope that belongs to your call, one Lord, one faith, one baptism, one God and Father of us all, who is above all and through all and in all. (Ephesians 4:1-6)

So how is it that the history of Christianity has been a history – long before the Reformation – of endless disagreements and arguments, typically resolving themselves into actual separation? Unpalatable as the truth may be, it is precisely the emphasis on unity that has been the cause of this. When so much emphasis is placed on the need for unity, the only way the prevailing notion can ever be questioned is by yet another breakaway; and no one of any sense is going to argue that questioning the prevailing notion is itself a kind of sinful breach of unity. If the notorious fissiparousness of Christianity is to be avoided, it must be recognized that Christians have a *right* – and often, indeed, a duty – to raise just such questions; and then to act upon them, because otherwise it is obvious that merely verbal questioning will simply be ignored. That is why the path that the Windsor Report recommends for healing the present division has to be opposed. The true solution is that evangelicals *must* accept that others, just as good Christians as themselves, nevertheless have a very different view of Christianity from theirs. The best definition of a Christian in the whole of the New Testament is Matthew 25:31-46, where there is no suggestion that Christians have to give an account of what they say or think, simply of what they do. If they are acting as Christians and claim to be Christians, then that is what they truly must be held to be.

Finally, the Report places great emphasis on what was agreed at the Lambeth Conference of 1998. This too has to be repudiated. Unofficially it already has been by a clear majority of Anglicans in North America, Britain, South Africa, Australia and

New Zealand; but the first, absolutely necessary step in healing present divisions is to repudiate it officially, and the sooner the better. This is not to impose any view of homosexuality on those other Churches where the attitudes of Western liberalism do not prevail (and may even be regarded with abhorrence); it is simply to make it quite clear that they can claim no right to impose their views on us. There is a telling passage in the Report on the subject of the introduction of Rites of Blessing for same-sex unions:

> In such circumstances, it should not be surprising that such developments are seen by some as surrendering to the spirit of the age rather than an authentic development of the gospel. (Para 142)

(As far as I can remember, this is the only actual mention of "the spirit of the age" anywhere in the Report; but the whole of it reads very much as a deliberate attempt to exorcise that particular demon.) There is in fact no necessary contradiction between "the spirit of the age" and "an authentic development of the gospel"; and the Church would do well openly to acknowledge its frequent indebtedness to the former in order to achieve the latter. It is "the spirit of the age" that the Church has to thank, times without number, for weaning it off its lamentable addiction to ancient cruelties: the persecution (and often burning) of witches and heretics, the upholding of slavery, the oppression of the Jews and of women; and last in line, still awaiting their redemption from Christian prejudice and hostility, the homosexuals. Even in those Western-minded Churches listed above, it is the change in the attitude of secular society that has forced a change in that of the Church; and to argue that for this very reason the Church should be resisting the change rather than adapting to it is merely stupidity masquerading as integrity. It is hard to doubt (despite the result of the recent American election) that the eventual acceptance of homosexuality, certainly throughout the West, will eventually be wider even than it is already, and all this was clear at the time of the Lambeth Conference; it was gross folly in the bishops, therefore, and particularly in Dr Carey (who was sufficiently familiar with the immediate situation to know better) to imagine they could obstruct the onward march of tolerance and understanding by an ecclesiastical fiat, however heavily supported.

Every one knew at the time that most of the southern bishops held different views on this subject from that of most of the northern ones; but it had never occurred, even to the southern bishops themselves, that they had the right to legislate for the communion as a whole until Dr Carey put the idea into their heads. In the Church of England itself, evangelicals made it perfectly clear that they were very displeased over the appointment of Dr David Jenkins as Bishop of Durham, but they claimed no right to ban it or to threaten that schism would be the result. This is the new development, inaugurated by Dr Carey and now reinforced by Dr Williams yielding to unwarranted pressure over the appointment of Jeffrey John to be Bishop of Reading, that must at all costs be resisted. And I do mean at all costs: if schism is the price of maintaining a liberal voice in the Church, then schism it will have to be.

D B Taylor is a graduate in theology, who worked for many years in an Oxford publishing house, and is now retired and living in North Wales.

THE SILENCING OF DEBATE

Gillian Cooke

[Note: The references in brackets, unless otherwise indicated, refer to the numbered paragraphs of The Windsor Report 2004.]

The task of the Lambeth Commission on Communion was to examine and report "on the legal and theological implications flowing from the decisions of the Episcopal Church (USA) [ECUSA] to appoint a priest in a committed same-sex relationship as one of its bishops, and of the Canadian Diocese of New Westminster (DNW) to authorize services for use in connection with same-sex unions," and specifically on "the canonical understandings of communion, impaired and broken communion...both within and between the Churches of the Anglican Communion" (p.13). It was required to make suggestions for maintaining the highest degree of communion possible. It was not part of its brief to consider the issues of human sexuality which had been discussed at previous Lambeth Conferences although, given the centrality of the issue in the present crisis, it can hardly be considered unimportant.

When discussing The Purposes and Benefits of Communion (Section A), the Report adopts a medical analogy of health and illness. Ephesians 2 pictures the Church as one body with Christ as its head; hence "health" for the Anglican Communion is as a "communion of Churches" nourished by the Holy Spirit. It states that there have been failures in the past, but does not identify these, preferring to concentrate on the positive results which led Anglicans "to embrace costly grace in standing together in opposition to racial enslavement and genocide," and to offer "aid to one another in combating famine, disease and the chaos caused by natural disasters"(9). These are all cited as positive examples of how the various Churches within the Anglican Communion, by a process of mutual discernment, have been concerned for other parts of "the body".

The disputes concerning the ordination of women did not alter this mutual concern, since the Instruments of Unity, i.e. the Archbishop of Canterbury, the Lambeth Conference, the Anglican Consultative Council and the Primates' Meeting, were all involved in the decision-making process. Provincial autonomy and interdependence were recognized. Division was avoided, even though there is a degree of impaired communion. (Some of us might, however, dispute the "health" image; too frequently it still seems like an all-male club congratulating themselves for including women, while women's views on how well the inclusion is working are not considered relevant to the debate. Furthermore, it seems to ignore much of the messiness of the conflict, which lasted over a century, as the Church began to include women in ministry, first as deaconesses and missionaries, until the beginning of their consecration as bishops.) Nevertheless, it can be seen that disagreements within the Anglican Communion on important matters do not necessarily lead to division, even though some of the Church's priests and bishops are not recognized by all parts of the Communion. Impaired communion is not the same as a total split in the Communion.

The current situation in the Communion is described in terms of "illness", with surface and deeper symptoms. Particular blame is laid on "synodical actions that have been taken in one diocese and one province, which have gone against both the letter and the spirit of the resolutions of the Lambeth Conference, reiterated as they are by the Primates' Meeting" (27). These, we are told, were seen by Anglican and other Christians to depart from "genuine apostolic faith" (28). These actions were greeted by declarations of impaired communion by some provinces, and by conservatives within the American and Canadian Churches, who, in some cases, sought episcopal oversight from other bishops. At no point in the Report is there a condemnation of those who threatened the life of Gene Robinson, who needed police protection and to wear a bulletproof vest for the consecration. Nor was there any condemnation of the abusive letters sent both to the Bishop of New Westminster and to Gene Robinson. There has been a constant misrepresentation of Gene Robinson's situation, describing him as "leaving his wife for another man," which was untrue. While taking part in a radio debate, I myself saw how reluctant conservatives can be to accept this; my conservative opponent repeated this lie and, although corrected by our interviewer, was unwilling to accept the truth. Furthermore, does defense of "the genuine apostolic faith" allow those (who admittedly may not have been members of the Church) to threaten the life of its leaders, to send abusive mail, and to slander their fellow believers? An unequivocal statement of condemnation of those who have done these things would have helped give substance to the statement that "any demonizing of homosexual persons, or their ill treatment, is totally against Christian charity" (146).

We are told that the Commission was not asked to continue the sexuality debate; but in referring to the Lambeth Conference resolution it would seem vital to look at this in its entirety, and at previous Conference resolutions on sexuality, all of which are given in the Report. The 1978 and 1988 reports both recognize the need for "deep and dispassionate study of the question of homosexuality, which would take seriously both the teaching of Scripture and the results of scientific and medical research" (pp.90 and 91). The 1988 resolution called "on each province to reassess, in the light of such study and because of our concern for human rights, its care for and attitude towards persons of homosexual orientation."

Are we supposed to believe that all provinces heeded this demand, and the more negative statements about homosexuality resulted from their reassessment in the light of study? Have the provinces considered the international scientific view that homosexuality is not a disease, but as normal a form of sexuality as heterosexuality? (Homosexuality was removed from the International Classification of Diseases in 1973.) Furthermore, how much have those who protested that ECUSA and DNW have gone against the Lambeth Declarations had an open dialogue with those who are gay and lesbian? The 1998 report committed the bishops "to listen to the experience of homosexual persons", and assures them that they are full members of the Body of Christ. It would seem to the present writer that the current crisis has happened because large parts of the Anglican Communion have chosen to ignore the commitments of the last three Lambeth Conference resolutions requesting study and dialogue. If Lambeth Resolutions are to be taken seriously, it is not logical simply to pick and choose parts of these with which to batter others, and ignore other parts.

It is not until paragraph 146 that we read, "The later sections of Lambeth Resolution 1.10 cannot be ignored more than the first section, as the Primates have noted." This is what has been argued here, yet it has been ignored by the Commission in diagnosing the "illness". It seems like an excuse to put off the debate indefinitely.

If an illness is to be successfully treated, it is essential to consider all the evidence, and not to jump to premature conclusions. It is a basic rule with first aid, where more than one casualty needs attention, to focus not on those making the most noise, but to attend first to those who are most silent, who are likely to be suffering more. The Commission has, I fear, been too concerned to satisfy those who shout loudest, while ignoring those in greatest need. The appropriateness of this analogy seems to be better than the superficial diagnosis of the Commission, where some inconvenient "symptoms" seem ignored, but were recognized by the Archbishop of Canterbury who, in the context of the Jeffrey John controversy, said he had been shocked by the ignorance about homosexuality. This is not surprising when we recognize how much silencing there has been.

In Britain most gay and lesbian people, if they have stayed in the Church, find it hard to speak up for fear of persecution. If they are clergy, they may be driven from their posts. But the situation is much worse in many parts of the world, and most frequently in those countries where bishops have been vociferously anti-gay in this present situation. Amnesty International and other human rights groups have documented the repressive legislation and human rights abuses in these countries; these include appalling tales of rape and murder. Nor are such acts of violence absent in Britain. As I write, yet another gay man, who had survived the bombing of a gay pub in Soho, has been murdered in London, and his companion injured in the attack. The British Home Office is concerned about violence against gay and lesbian people, and has introduced initiatives to confront this. We often hear of the brave acts by the Confessing Church in Germany against anti-Semitism, but the Churches so often forget that gay people were also victims of the holocaust, and many thousands died. The Jewish holocaust alerted the Church to the dangers of anti-Semitism, which had been so long endorsed by linking the Jews to the death of Christ. Christians may not themselves carry out violence, but their past attitude to the Jewish people, and their present condemnation of gay and lesbian people and failure to condemn the violence, gives comfort to those who do.

What is also being silenced is the voice of medicine and science. As has already been mentioned, homosexuality was removed from the International Classification of Diseases in 1973, yet nowhere in the Church of England's lengthy discussion document, "Some Issues in Human Sexuality" (Church House Publishing, 2003), which is offered to Christians as a resource to help discussion in line with the Lambeth Resolution, do we find this mentioned. If the demands of the earlier Lambeth Conference resolutions had been taken seriously, those producing the document would have ensured that they did include the best and most recent information concerning the development of sexuality, whether heterosexual or homosexual. The bishops had a duty to gain the best information from the Royal College of Psychiatrists, but did not do this. Indeed, if it was considered important to have contributions from the President of the World Bank and the Prime Minister, Tony Blair, on the subject of world poverty and debt at the last Lambeth Conference, would not a lecture from an eminent psychiatrist on the subject of sexuality have helped inform the debate on this subject? Without an accurate scientific input, the Churches are basing their debates on pre-scientific views.

In the section "Illness: The Deeper Symptoms" we are

told about the failings of the ECUSA and the Diocese of New Westminster with regard to their part in the Anglican Communion. It is hard to escape the conclusion that they are condemned, because it is easy to ignore the latter parts of the Lambeth Resolution when it is merely a discussion with words, and much harder when, as now, the Communion is forced to face the issue as one concerned with real people and their lives.

We are reminded in the Report that not all theological developments are right; that some differences within Anglicanism are *adiaphora* (meaning "things that do not make a difference"), but that controversial matters go beyond the limits of subsidiarity, and need deciding at a Communion-wide level. Crucial to the Report's argument are the demands of the Virginia Report (1977), and included in the 1998 Lambeth Conference Report), confirmed by the Anglican Consultative Council in 2002, that questions which concern all the Churches of the Anglican Communion need to involve the Lambeth Conference, the ACC and the Primates' Meeting. The reason for the present crisis is that "it appears to the wider Communion that neither the DNW nor ECUSA has made a serious attempt to offer an explanation to, or consult meaningfully with, the Communion as a whole about the significant development of theology which alone could justify the recent moves by a diocese or province" (33).

Has the Communion forgotten that the early Church's admission of Gentiles (Acts 15) only happened after Paul and Barnabas had, without consultation, baptized Gentiles? This scandalized some Jewish worshippers, who persecuted the apostles and drove them out of Antioch. The knowledge that the Holy Spirit was active in those who had previously been excluded was part of the evidence on which decisions were made for inclusion. Gay and lesbian clergy have contributed richly to the Church for many years, but the Lambeth Commission seem reluctant to consider this type of evidence in the present situation. (Indeed, the offer by Gene Robinson to speak to the Commission was refused, and he was told that the debate was not personal, although he was clearly referred to in its Mandate.) Many can bear witness to the fact that the fruits of the Spirit are as visible in homosexual clergy as in their heterosexual colleagues. One can only wonder how the Church would look today, if the Lambeth Commission had been asked to decide on the admission of Gentiles almost two thousand years ago!

Probably few of us had noticed, but suddenly we now seem to have a centralizing of authority, which seems a dangerous development. The remainder of the Report would seem to strengthen this tendency.

Marilyn McCord Adams highlights the dangers of this process that would change the Anglican Communion from a "loose federation of legally independent Churches" to one which more closely resembles the "coercive and authoritarian structures of Rome" as enshrined in canon law (*Church Times* 29th October 2004, page 9, article "How to Quench the Spirit"). She states that "Jesus' inaugural sermon and his Synoptic Gospel ministry suggest that "release for the captive" may well involve the undoing of long-standing taboos." Examples of these can be found in the gospels, in history and in our newspapers; and even when changes take place among those of similar background, "fresh consensus on issues of race, gender and sex is the work of decades." She fears that "the structures proposed in the Windsor report invite those who want to stop the process of change, before it reshapes the Church, to appeal for allies from other cultures where the taboos are still firmly in place. It contains no comparable provision for individual and Communion-wide self-examination; no provision for systematically exhorting member Churches to uproot taboos that oppress."

The structures referred to by McCord Adams have evolved gradually through the history of the Anglican Communion, and are referred to as a whole as the "Instruments of Unity". Probably most of us feel like the two bewildered laymen and one clergyman in St Gargoyle's cartoon (*Church Times* 29th October 2004), who are holding an extraordinary musical instrument, comprising a mish-mash of many orchestral instruments. The caption reads, "Nobody actually knew what an Instrument of Unity was." The Report does tell us what the Instruments of Unity are: the Archbishop of Canterbury, the Lambeth Conference, the Anglican Consultative Council and the Primates' Meeting. These have evolved historically as the Church of England spread overseas, as the contribution of lay people grew in the government of the Churches, and the international nature of the Communion developed. Until now these "Instruments" have acted largely in a consultative and informal way. While the Instruments as now proposed may lead to less confusion than St Gargoyle's cartoon, it is questionable whether they can bring unity out of discord.

The Commission now proposes to change these from being consultative and informal, to something with legal status. The role of the Archbishop of Canterbury would be strengthened, and he would have a Council of Advice to further strengthen his position in dealing with Communion-wide matters. I think that many of us rejoiced when Rowan Williams became the Archbishop of Canterbury, since he was clearly a man of sincere faith and intellectual stature and, as is important in the present situation, one who was well informed about sexuality. Indeed, he himself suffered abuse and an undermining of his authority because of his views. Subsequently, however, I think many of us fear that pressure from conservative advisors, possibly from those appointed by his conservative predecessor, have limited his ability to lead the Church to face the issues in an informed and open way. Given the bias of the Report, there seems a real danger that a Council of Advice would be a further containment of the Archbishop to ensure that conservatives can continue to silence informed debate.

Another development would be an Anglican Covenant which each member Church would be expected to sign. Much of its suggested content is something which most Anglicans would be happy to sign, and reflects the Lambeth Quadrilateral, i.e. that the essentials of Anglican Unity are Holy Scripture, the Apostles' and Nicene Creeds, the Sacraments of Baptism and Holy Communion and the historic episcopate. However, some clauses give cause for concern, especially as they are interpreted in the present Report.

Conservatives and liberals both claim the support of Scripture, and the Report recognizes that there will be differences in the reading of Scripture, including some, which come from different traditions in the Church, and others which arise because of local culture. The claim, however, that, "Within the Communion we have developed theological and practical ways ... of distinguishing acceptable and unacceptable forms of diversity." gives cause for concern. Since the Report is very much on the side of the conservatives, it is certainly not recognizing diversity; it is hard to escape the conclusion that liberal biblical interpretation, which recognizes the varied developments in Biblical Studies, is being silenced.

We are reminded that "the divine call to communion is inviolable, and no member Church may declare unilaterally irreversible broken communion with another" (Article 6, p.82). This is a commendable demand, which few liberals would dispute. Furthermore, few liberals would want to question the demand that, "no member Church shall act without consideration of the common good of the Communion" (Article 9 (1), p.83). However, in the demand that provinces should not act on controversial matters until there is agreement, we need to ask, "Who decides what is controversial?" I am reminded of my Free Church childhood, where one faithful Christian man regularly harangued the congregation about the evils of attending football matches. He was sincere, but should the fact he felt offended lead us to forbid attendance at football matches? It is one thing to take him seriously as a person, but another to allow his views to condemn all those Christians who attend football matches – including Archbishop Carey, who was a keen football fan.

The crucial question concerns which differences between Christians are essential or not essential. Some differences can be tolerated (these are not specified), while others are clearly wrong and must be resisted – racism and child abuse are given as examples. Such issues now seem obvious, but this has not always been the case. Racism underlay colonialism, slavery and apartheid, and continued for centuries unchallenged by the Church, which could cite Biblical authority for the acceptance of slavery, as did the Dutch Reformed Church in its backing for apartheid.

The extent and damage done by child abuse has only recently been recognized. The Churches of all denominations are now painfully aware that many children have been abused by clergy and other religious leaders who were trusted, but this awareness is recent. In the past, children were punished for lying when they told adults they had been abused; and when families supported their abused children, the family might be ostracized by that religious community. They were usually accused of slandering good, faithful Christian men, and damaging the good name of the Church. Not only were the victims silenced by those who abused them, but power within the Churches was used to reinforce the silencing. We are only now discovering the extent of this misuse of power to silence victims. We need also to recognize that power within the Church can be used to silence other oppressed groups.

The Report claims that "that which embodies and expresses renewed humanity in Christ is always mandatory for Christians" (90). This is clearly not in dispute, but Judæo-Christian history is full of examples, which demonstrate the inability of the people of God to see those whom it excludes, or to attend to those whose message it does not want to hear. The Old Testament prophets spoke out forcefully when the people of God congratulated themselves because of their religious practices but were blind and deaf to those in need around them. Prophets who preached this message might be told to go away and be quiet by the religious leaders of the time (e.g. Amos 7:12-13). Stephen sums it up in Acts 7, when he asks his accusers, "Can you name a single prophet your ancestors never persecuted?" The history of the Church has countless other examples, yet the Report shows no awareness of the danger that the Church might fail to recognize new insights which the Spirit reveals.

We are told that even where Christians have a free choice, they should avoid giving offence to weaker Christians, who may be drawn into sin (93). Here, although it is not specified, it is assumed that ECUSA and the DNW should hold back (even if they are right) from offending those who disagree. However, this analogy seems to be a false one. In Romans 14 Paul is referring to dietary laws; he is not referring to how we treat other human beings. The New Testament is quite clear about our responsibility to love our neighbor. The Commission members do not seem to have noticed that many of Jesus' actions regarding love of neighbor caused great offence to some of his fellow Jews, and that his harshest words were to those who considered themselves "righteous"; their concern for the Law constricted their perception of "neighbor" because they saw many ordinary people as "sinners".

The dangers of the centralized authority envisaged in the Covenant become even clearer, however, with regard to Articles 13 Ministerial Obligations of Unity, 16 The Bonds of Mutual Loyalty, Part IV Exercise of Autonomy in Communion, and Part V Management of Communion Issues. Under Article 13 each minister, particularly a bishop, is to be a visible sign of unity, maintaining communion both within each Church and with Canterbury and other Churches within the Anglican Communion. "No minister, especially a bishop, shall: (a) act without due regard to, or jeopardize the unity of, the Communion ... (c) unreasonably be the cause or focus of division and strife in their Church, or elsewhere in the Communion; (d) if in episcopal office, unreasonably refuse any invitation to attend meetings of the Instruments of Unity" (p.84).

On the surface the demands are unremarkable, but the Report makes clear that ECUSA and the DNW would be clear examples of what is in mind here, and that Gene Robinson is a cause and focus of division. In short, the Covenant would effectively provide a veto to any member Church, which decided that they did not want a particular bishop or archbishop for some reason, so long as they could claim that such an appointment offended their conscience.

This seems to set a dangerous precedent. We should not forget that the present Archbishop of Canterbury was the subject of abuse by many conservatives in the Church of England, who refused to allow him to speak at their conference after his appointment, and considered that a mistake had been made in allowing Archbishop Hope to speak at the same conference. Is this why the Archbishop of Canterbury needs a Council of Advice? Is it to rein in an Archbishop of Canterbury who is seen by some to be dangerously liberal but someone they cannot just get rid of? Effectively, since liberals do not want to exclude conservatives from the Church, conservatives alone would use the opportunity to object to the appointment of any liberal bishop. There is no place here for a member Church to act prophetically, because someone could claim to be offended.

The Report also outlines procedures aimed at healing the current divisions in the Communion, and we again see a bias in favor of conservatives. Conservative bishops who have intervened in other provinces, dioceses and parishes are asked to express regret, affirm their desire to remain in the Communion, and to cease further interventions (155). It is interesting to note that the Report recognizes they may have felt "a conscientious duty" to have done what they did. There is, however, no suggestion that they should not be invited to future Lambeth Conferences and other Communion-wide events. Indeed, as the Covenant proposes (Article 13d), bishops should not "unreasonably refuse any invitation to attend meetings of the Instruments of Unity."

On the other hand, ECUSA is blamed for the "hurt and offence caused by their actions"; there is no recognition that they may have felt a "conscientious duty" in carrying out their actions. They are asked to regret breaching "the bonds of affection" by electing and consecrating Gene Robinson, and for "the consequences that followed"; these actions would "represent the desire of the ECUSA to remain within the Communion." Pending this, all those involved in the consecration of Gene Robinson "should be invited to consider in all conscience whether they should withdraw themselves from representative functions in the Anglican Communion". They are also asked for a moratorium on the election and consecration of any future candidates who are "living in a same-gender union, until some new consensus in the Anglican Communion emerges" (134). In contrast to the norm of all bishops being required to attend

Communion-wide events (Article 13(d) of the Covenant), those bishops linked to the election and consecration of Gene Robinson are required to consider absenting themselves. Furthermore, the suggestion that "considerable caution" be exercised in inviting Gene Robinson to the councils of the Communion would indicate that the Commission wish him to be excluded. Clearly the Covenant is not intended to unify differing viewpoints, but to exclude dissent.

It would perhaps be apposite to point out that the creation of provincial episcopal visitors was never discussed by the Anglican Communion, but there have been no suggestions that they be excluded from the Lambeth Conference. Many in the Church of England see them as extremely divisive, and would like to see the Act of Synod that created them, abolished. Again, they represent a generous accommodation of conservative opinion, which is not matched by concern for the consciences of those who want an inclusive Church (in this case inclusive of women).

The failure of conservatives to recognize the consciences of those wanting change is very different to the attitude of liberals who press for change. This can be seen most clearly when we look at ECUSA's own statements. They declared in 1976 that "homosexual persons are children of God who have a full and equal claim with all other persons upon the love, acceptance, and pastoral concern and care of the Church." No one could accuse ECUSA, however, of promoting promiscuity for gay and lesbian people; those "in monogamous, non-celibate unions" are expected to show "fidelity, monogamy, mutual affection and respect, careful, honest communication, and the holy love, which enables those in such relationships to see in each other the image of God." They acknowledge that "such relationships exist throughout the Church," and are giving Christian guidance. However, their statement of 2003 makes it clear that they recognize a diversity of views, and differences in pastoral practice. There is no wish to exclude anyone, including conservatives, and in 2004 ECUSA declared they would make every effort to ensure that alternative episcopal oversight would be provided in situations where bishops and clergy/congregations were divided. The Church of Canada has made similar commitments about episcopal oversight. The Canadian Church has deferred a province-wide acceptance of same-sex blessings until 2007, but meanwhile is allowing them if a diocese wishes to introduce them. It is also continuing debate on human sexuality and "intentionally involving gay and lesbian persons" (pp.97-8 and 101-6).

We can clearly see the huge gulf between the attitudes of conservatives and liberals. Conservatives wish to exclude those with whom they do not agree, while liberals wish to include all, recognizing that none of us has the whole truth. Surely, if there are true bonds of affection, listening to the other, even when we do not necessarily agree, must work two ways. It also needs to be recognized that liberals, as well as conservatives, have consciences. It is hard to escape the conclusion that what is being offered in the proposals for Maintenance of Communion, and in the Anglican Covenant, would effectively outlaw a pro-gay voice in the highest authorities of the Church, while conservatives would be free to express their views, even when they are based on ignorance, lies and misrepresentation.

In conclusion, we must ask what has happened to the demand that the Commission make suggestions for maintaining the highest degree of communion possible. Rather than do this, we have been offered a model which excludes those who want change. There seems no concern that the Anglican Communion might thereby not hear what the Spirit is saying at the beginning of the 21st century.

Rowan Williams (as Bishop of Monmouth), in his lecture

"Making Moral Decisions" to the Lambeth Conference in 1998, warned that a desire for "'purity" could lead to sacrificing the insights of others with whom we disagreed. Rather than think about sexuality, he asked his listeners to consider the differences between Christians regarding "the manufacture and retention of weapons of mass destruction," to which he had long been opposed. He states, "I cannot at times believe we are reading the same Bible," but he recognizes that in a violent world "the question of how we take responsibility for each other, how we avoid a bland and uncostly withdrawal from the realities of our environment, is not easily or quickly settled." He reminds Christians that in the Body of Christ they are united not only with the present but with the past, with "those who justified slavery, torture or the execution of heretics on the basis of the same Bible as the one I read, who prayed more intensely than I ever shall." He stresses that "unity at all costs is indeed not a Christian goal; our unity is "Christ-shaped", or it is empty." Nevertheless, "so long as we have a language in common and the "grammar of obedience" in common, we have, I believe, to turn away from the temptation to seek the purity and assurance of a community speaking with only one voice, and to embrace the reality of living in a communion that is fallible and divided" (Lambeth Conference Report 1998, pp.334-44).

Rowan Williams was not suggesting that anything goes in the making of moral decisions, but recognizing that Christians are influenced in their beliefs by their culture, whether this is geographical or at different points in history. The concern for "purity" can impede the search for spiritual insights by creating artificial barriers that cut us off from other Christians, and from the insights they have gained and can share with us.

Finally we may ask whether the Commission has indeed helped restore the Anglican Communion to health. I fear not.

The Communion seems to be becoming an emaciated, exclusive sect, silencing debate on Biblical interpretation, ignoring the developments in scientific knowledge, and silencing the voices of those it wishes to exclude. The Lambeth resolutions on sexuality have called for study, dialogue and debate; but those who have shouted loudest want none of this, and the Communion would seem to have given them what they wanted.

The Revd Gillian Cooke is an Anglican priest who has worked as a chaplain in higher education, industry, prisons, and to Rampton Hospital.

TREASURE IN
EARTHEN VESSELS

Anthony Woollard

The current debate in the Anglican Communion can be looked at on various levels. At one level, it is about how decisions should be taken within the Church – and whether, by "Church", one means a parish, a diocese, a national organization, an international Communion or indeed the whole fellowship of Christians. At another, it is about the factors that should be taken into account in making those decisions, and specifically decisions about matters of sexual ethics and discipline. I want to look at these from the point of view of a layman – a theologically trained layman, it is true, but now essentially a "person in the pew" with an interest in both questions. As a Diocesan Synod member, the question of *structures* of authority and decision-making is of concern to me. As a member of the Centre for the Study of Christianity and Sexuality I am at least equally concerned about the *basis* on which decisions, specifically in the area of sexuality, should be taken.

I begin with the structural issue. Christians are, and have

always been, divided about many matters. Sometimes, as in the Great Schism of 1054 and again at the Reformation and subsequently, that has led to separation. At other times, as in the great Councils of the Church, there has been a search for consensus, with more or less satisfactory results for most of the Church, but all too often at the price of excluding some.

At other times again there has been a policy of "live and let live". For example, unless one considers it as one factor in the formation of the Society of Friends or the Mennonites, the issue of pacifism has never led to schism, even though some Christians would argue that it is quite a feature of New Testament teaching. On the whole, the matters which have led either to schism or to painful consensus have been issues about the nature of God, of Christ or of the means of salvation, or else issues about the fundamental ordering of the Church itself; and, rightly or wrongly, pacifism has not been generally seen as being in this category.

Mention of the Friends however reminds me that they, more than any other tradition within Christianity, have held to the ideal of reaching decisions by consensus. No votes are ever taken in a Friends meeting. In theory, therefore, there is protection against the "tyranny of the majority", and nothing new can happen until everyone is persuaded. The desirability of such an approach is readily seen, since, if it works, it means that the whole Body of Christ is behind the decision and there are no disgruntled minorities.

The trouble of course is that this approach, even assuming that it genuinely works, can inhibit change. It also sits uneasily with a different dimension of decision making within the Christian tradition: the role of prophecy. Isaiah and Jeremiah did not wait for a community consensus before expressing prophetic teachings – and prophetic actions. Many Christian individuals and groups have felt called to act prophetically at various times in the Church's history on various issues, not least the issue of war and peace and other social matters. And the Church's history would be infinitely less rich if they had not done so.

As I have followed the present debate, I could not help being reminded of St Augustine's prophetic stand against the Donatists, and also of that Article of the Church of England which insists that the unworthiness of ministers does not hinder the effect of the Sacrament. Neither Augustine nor the Thirty-Nine Articles are amongst my favorite sources of authority, but they may be relevant here.

The Donatists insisted that no one could minister in the Church who had committed apostasy during the great persecutions of the third century. They could quote Scripture in their defense. Certain passages, notably in the Letter to the Hebrews (10:26-27), speak of apostasy as the unforgivable sin. Augustine however, for all his own authoritarian and dualistic tendencies, could see that such a stand denied the Grace of God, which could work even through the most unworthy of ministers: "treasure in earthen vessels" as St Paul puts it (2 Corinthians 4:7). And at the Reformation the Church of England, to its eternal credit, took a similar stand against the extreme reformers who would impose a "worthiness test" on ministers of the Gospel, and indeed on church members.

Today we are faced with a situation in which some parts of our Communion would reject as "unworthy" those ministers whose life does not conform to a particular understanding of the Christian sexual lifestyle. They can quote Scripture in their defense. They are as happy as the Donatists were to excommunicate those parts of the Communion which happen to disagree with them.

Augustine might have said that, in order to appease the

Donatists' tender consciences, the Church should impose a rigorist discipline until it had achieved agreement on a more generous approach. (He could have quoted St Paul in support.) Or he might have proposed a compromise, in which open breach of communion was avoided, but steps were taken to discourage "unworthy" bishops from attending the Church's synods and councils, and a moratorium was placed upon their further recognition within their local churches.

He did not do so. He took a firm stand against Donatism and all its works. We may at times feel that Augustine has been a baleful influence on some aspects of the Church's understanding of sin and especially in the area of sexuality. But on this particular matter we must give the most profound thanks for the stand he took. Without it, many of us would probably not be within the household of faith today.

Waiting for consensus, then, may seem like a good thing in principle, but may not always be right in practice. Large parts of the Anglican Communion refused to wait for consensus on the ordained ministry of women. (The Report of the Windsor Commission rather glosses over this fact; most of the involvement of our Communion's "instruments of unity" with this issue has in fact addressed *faits accomplis*.) They thereby put the unity of the Body under strain, and that strain remains in places and has been mitigated by uneasy compromises. Yet we can already see the fruits of those prophetic actions. In my own Diocese of Coventry the ministry of women is almost universally accepted, and is manifestly vital (women already form a majority of ordinands). And that pattern can be repeated in many dioceses across the whole Communion. It has often, and rightly, required a struggle for consensus at the *parochial* level where a woman priest may take time to be fully accepted. But at higher levels within the organization, decisions have been taken by large majorities, and, to most of us, the good fruits of those decisions are becoming clearer by the day.

It is probably true that only a few parts of the Communion can, as yet, take similar majority decisions regarding the acceptance of gay and lesbian clergy. This is despite the fact that such clergy are already ministering in substantial numbers, and again (I speak very personally here) the special fruits of their ministry are evident to those who have eyes to see. It is also true that the question of women *bishops* remains unresolved in the Church of England for the moment, and there is perhaps a case for saying that the bishop, as the focus of unity, may need to be subject to more rigorous rules of acceptability than apply to ordinary clergy. So we cannot simply say that the lessons of the struggle for women's ordination should be applied to the "problem" of certain national churches, which are willing to consecrate gay bishops. Yet the underlying question – that of the validity of the prophetic action which goes against a current consensus – still seems to me to be relevant.

A prophetic action also seems to me to have greater validity the higher up the hierarchy it occurs. The Anglican Communion is certainly an inherently episcopal Church. A bishop with his (or her) diocese can properly take a prophetic action regarding church order which could not be taken at parochial level, and that can be powerful and valid. But where, as in the USA, that action is taken in a national synod, it would seem to be even more powerful and valid. The Windsor Report demonstrates that that process was not quite as straightforward as outside observers may have imagined; and, in particular, that there was considerable caution amongst the bishops themselves and their theological advisers. But the story of the ordination of women priests, and later of the consecration of women bishops, is not dissimilar. Advice is given; a synod acts; prophecy is uttered.

Of course, the wider Communion is not bound to respond positively to any and every prophetic action. Many individual Christians and Christian groups have had to suffer for their prophecies, as a necessary stage before those prophecies began to enjoy some acceptance. But the Anglican tradition generally has been more Gamaliel-like, prepared to wait and see, to live and let live, until the truth of a prophecy is clear. The Windsor Commission provides evidence that this has happened, at the global level, even in the controversial matter of women bishops. If there is now to be any sort of departure from that approach, – let us all be clear – this is not, in church-order terms, a reaffirmation of the tradition, but a deliberate change in it.

Let me turn now to the underlying question about the authority for Christian sexual ethics. The Commission was, strictly speaking, focused not on this but on issues of church order. Yet all of those involved in the debate are concerned first and foremost about this deeper issue.

The Donatists could quote Scripture in support of their views on apostasy as something which made it impossible to minister in the Church. If you take a certain view of Scripture, there is little doubt what the relevant passages say, and little possibility of explaining them away. It would have been surprising if the early Church had *not* had a horror of apostasy. Yet Augustine was courageous enough to say that a rigorous use of such Biblical witness denied the Grace of God.

The various Scriptural texts about sexuality, and specifically about homosexuality, come into much the same category. Many attempts have been made to show that the Biblical horror at certain kinds of sexual irregularity is not quite what it appears to be. For example, it may well be that the main focus of attention on "homosexuality", in both Old and New Testaments, is actually cultic male prostitution in pagan temples, or the semi-ritualized (and in today's terms possibly pedophiliac) relationships of the Greek gymnasium. These are clearly very different from some of the stable, egalitarian and spiritually nourishing gay and lesbian relationships which, at their best, we can encounter today. And it may well also be true that the very concept of "homosexuality" is something far too recent to be compared with the anxiety in Biblical times about "acting against nature", and that that anxiety has more to do with culturally determined fears about effeminacy in men. These arguments need to be taken much more seriously by those who promote "the clear meaning of Scripture". But I am not sure how far you can take them. There is a general tenor in much (though not all) of the Bible which treats sexual "irregularity" in general, and same-sex relationships in particular, as a grave danger for the people of God.

And so it is. Sex is dangerous. Heterosexual penetrative sex, where it is pre- or extra-marital, raises serious issues about pregnancy, family stability and inheritance. Acceptance of same-sex relationships (and quite a few heterosexual practices), on the other hand, raises questions about humans' duty to "increase and multiply". Some of these questions may be looked at very differently in a radically different social context – though the matter of family stability, at least, is of perennial concern. But there are some more general elements of "threat" within human sexuality, which explain why this topic is so explosive in the sensitivities of many Christians. It is an area where self-seeking and self-gratification, power relationships, and the possibility of a very secular ecstasy may seem to threaten the deepest ideals of Christian spirituality. The attraction of celibacy, at certain stages in the Church's history, is only too understandable – in which case procreative married sex becomes a necessary evil, and all other kinds of sex simply evil.

A short essay such as this is no place to try to explore all the inadequacies of such an approach. Part of it, I would argue, reflects serious deficiencies in the Church's theology of creation. How do we reconcile these strictures with the fact that humans appear to be created to behave in a way that does not fit neatly into Christian spirituality? Do we just put down to Original Sin or the Devil all those forces in human experience which seem to be about self-seeking, power and the rest? This issue is massively important not just in the area of sexuality. The Rabbis spoke of the "evil inclination" which gives rise to aggression and competition as well as to the sexual appetite – in fact, most of the drivers of human progress as well as most of the occasions of sin. Unlike many Christian theologians, however, they accepted this as part of the order of creation, and did not condemn human beings for being human. We are in deep territory here, but I suggest we may have something to learn from the Rabbis.

The Church – even, to some extent, the Roman Catholic Church – has already accepted the importance of the non-procreative dimensions within human sexuality. They may be a puzzle to some natural law theorists, but our modern experience, with cultural and scientific developments, has led us to recognize their power. They are all the more important in a new world, far removed from the Biblical one, in which old bonds of community have broken down and individuals seek some form of fulfillment which will both give to, and receive from, "the other". In 1930 our own Lambeth Conference took its landmark decision to approve contraception as a way of making relational sex possible (within marriage) without the constant fear of pregnancy. Most of us are too young to remember how revolutionary that was, though Roman Catholics can still understand its dramatic significance. Might we hope, and work, for a similar change regarding homosexuality? If so, how and when? And how would we expect the Church to deal with the cry of "How long, O Lord?" in the meantime?

Clearly we cannot hope to develop Anglican understanding without an appeal to the sources of that understanding. Authority within Anglicanism is traditionally supposed to rest upon the "tripod" of Scripture, tradition, and reason. So far as we can see, and despite the possibility of some more liberal interpretations, both Scripture and tradition seem deeply suspicious of homosexuality. But they were also seen, until recently, as opposing contraception, albeit less explicitly. In past times they have been seen (and this really is rather explicit) as condemning the loan of money on interest, and many other practices which are now generally accepted as no bar to Church membership and Christian ministry. It would seem that the third leg of the tripod – reason – has been quite influential, especially in more recent times. Is this, then, the source from which a new understanding of homosexuality could come?

The concept of reason as a source of Christian authority is a very contested one, because in the past it has often been captured by the idea of "natural law". Natural law is a very slippery eel indeed when it comes to sexuality. It has historically been used to demonstrate that, biologically, sex is intended for the sole purpose of procreation. It has also been used to justify the dominance of men over women, which has given rise to all sorts of difficulties. The same natural law theory which has been so emphatic about the procreative nature of sexuality has also – in defiance of "the clear meaning of Scripture" – in past times been used to justify prostitution as a necessary evil, on the grounds that human males demonstrably need more sexual outlets than the bonds of procreative marriage can offer. The same approach today, taking into account the "sperm wars" debate for example, could be used (though so far as I know it has not) to justify both male and female promiscuity in a natural effort to optimize genetic outcomes! The one thing that a natural-law approach does seem to demonstrate is that sex in humans is always much more complex than appears at first sight.

Today, particularly amongst gay and lesbian Christians, there is more emphasis on *experience*, either as an aspect of reason or as a fourth leg of the seat of authority. The Gospel promise that "you will know them by their fruits" (Matthew 7:20) does seem to justify a more experiential approach to authority than most rule-bound systems admit. Yet there is no need to rehearse the problems of an excessive reliance on personal experience, particularly in cases where the majority, however empathetic, can never share that experience. The Windsor Report reminds the Communion in the strongest possible terms of the absolute need to listen to the experience of gays and lesbians; but it is all too easy to dismiss that experience as "merely subjective", and it may be a very long time before the authentic stories of lesbian and gay Christians attract the deep response throughout the Church that they deserve.

As I look at all this confusion – and not least the gap between "the clear teaching of Scripture" and aspects of my own experience as a 21st-century heterosexual man (let alone anyone else's) – I am forced to conclude that *the sources of Christian authority are themselves, like those who minister them, "earthen vessels".* They simply do not provide "answers". The Truth of God is often refracted very brightly through the sources of authority; it *is* possible for us to "walk in the light of life". Nevertheless, to us mortals it comes refracted, not direct. Sometimes it may call us to take a prophetic stand. But always it should move us to humility in our dealings with those with whom we disagree, and particularly with those who claim to have glimpsed new images in the refractions.

Which takes us back to Gamaliel. *If this enterprise is of human origin it will break up of its own accord; but if it does in fact come from God, you will not only be unable to destroy them, but you might find yourselves fighting against God* (Acts 5:38-39). Part of the genius of Anglicanism is that it has historically recognized the wisdom of those words, from Elizabeth I's refusal to "open a window into men's souls" to the present day. Its excursions into heresy and witch-hunting have been rare and short. Within the 20th century it accepted new insights and/or tolerated differences on issues as various as aspects of fundamental doctrine (the 1938 report and more recently *Christian Believing*); contraception (already cited) and much more recently divorce and remarriage; church order and ecumenical relationships (the Church of South India saga); and, last but not least, the ordained ministry of women. True, on many of these it sought to retain some limits and compromises, and often the solution has been a bit of a fudge. The Windsor Report itself is something of a fudge and could probably not have been otherwise. But 20th-century Anglicanism, taken all in all, has a record of liberality and generosity that accords fully with Augustine's stress on the primacy of Grace. If in the 21st century that were to be lost, through a continued rejection of lesbian and gay Christians and the Churches which affirm them, then we might well ask whether the Anglican Communion in its current form would still be capable of witnessing authentically to the Gospel of Grace.

Anthony Woollard is a member of the Council of the Modern Church-people's Union, and also of the Committee of the Centre for the Study of Christianity and Sexuality, whose newsletter he edits.

INCLUSIVENESS AND UNITY

Jonathan Clatworthy

There is no reason at all why the Anglican Communion should split over an ethical issue like homosexuality. Christians have always disagreed over a great many ethical issues, but they are no cause to split institutions. What *would* justify a split would be if it cannot decide how to organize itself and make decisions.

This is the real issue. Currently the noisiest debate is over gay bishops; yet when we listen to what is being said, the ethics of homosexuality – analyses of Biblical texts, or the Christian tradition, or psychological research on gay orientation – have not been front page news. Instead we have heard many claims to "the plain truth" and "the Bible's teaching", spiced with accusations of disloyalty. Anglicanism currently sounds less like a truth-seeking community sharing insights with each other, and more like a collection of divergent traditions which only enter the forum of Anglican debate after their own mind has been made up. It is as though we already have two competing Anglican Communions. How has this come about?

I was the son of an Anglo-Catholic vicar who disagreed with Protestants, but never doubted that they were Christians. On going to university in the 1960s, I was astonished to find myself denounced as a non-Christian by the Christian Union, who even sent a delegate to spend an evening convincing me. Christian Union meetings were on Saturdays as, apparently, the Bible forbade alcohol, and therefore Christians did not go to parties.

Back in a university in the 1980s as a chaplain, I found the leaders of comparable groups had moved on: Christians were by this time permitted alcohol, but much effort was spent in debates with the Student Union over their abortion policies. The big no-no was now abortion. Again I was apparently not a Christian, this time because chaplains never were.

Now the successors of those groups have moved on to homosexuality. From people who claim to believe in the supreme authority of Scripture, this makes a very odd list indeed. Alcohol and drunkenness are well known to the authors of the Bible, but it never recommends total abstinence. Abortion gets not a single mention in Holy Writ, despite being practised in the ancient Near East. Homosexuality does better, with a minimum of three Biblical condemnations, and a possible maximum of seven. This means that most Biblical authors do not mention the matter at all, and those who do only give us a sentence or two on it.

All these campaigns have been very common in Churches claiming allegiance to the Bible; so why a constant succession of major ethical campaigns, and why these? Within student culture it is easy to see what function they perform. The leaders, anxious to maintain their membership, emphasize the starkness of the difference between Christians and non-Christians. This simple division of the human race into black and white encourages members to believe they belong to a minority of the saved, radically different from the unsaved outsiders. Since in reality they are not much different from other people, they need some symbol to reassure them of their distinctiveness. The cheapest, least demanding symbol is to focus on a single ethical issue which is characteristically theirs.

This sectarian sense of distinctiveness was for a long time contrary to the Anglican tradition; recently things have changed. I was ordained in the mid-1970s. Some of my contemporaries so disdained Anglicanism that they avoided calling themselves "Church of England curates", preferring to think of themselves as "Christian ministers who happen to be paid by the Church of England". Some of these are now in senior positions – perhaps even bishops – but today, instead of being embarrassed by their Anglican identity, they are claiming the titles of "orthodox" and "mainstream". It is not that they have abandoned their disdain for the Anglicanism of the 1970s; instead they are claiming that their distinctive ethos, which then was outside mainstream Anglicanism, now represents true Anglicanism. To make this claim may not seem to them to be a takeover bid, but in fact it is.

Underlying the current debate, therefore, lie two mutually exclusive accounts of Christian theology and the Church. Is the individual Christian free to explore the nature of religious truth, or obliged to believe exactly what the Church leaders decree? Should the Church include a wide range of people who want to belong, or should it exlude those who do not meet sharply defined standards of doctrine and morals?

Within Christianity, the disagreement between these two has always existed. The early Catholics against the Gnostics, Augustine against the Donatists, the magisterial Reformers against the radical Reformers, all faced the demand for a "pure" Church, cleansed of those not up to the mark. According to the gospels, there were similar debates between Jesus and the Pharisees.

Why have we spent so much of our history arguing like this? Cannot both sides put their reasons in the public domain and try to reach agreement? No; and to make matters worse, the very idea of reasoned public debate about doctrine is itself under dispute. According to one view, any attempt to apply rational processes to Christian doctrine would be to submit supreme truth to mere human reason. Instead the individual Christian should just receive the truth directly from divine revelation, the content of which some people happen to know with a certainty transcending the mere opinions of others.

How has Christianity produced this absurd situation? Many Christians are taught to take such attitudes for granted, as though they were the obvious way to proceed. In fact, however, they have a history. Like all Christian doctrines, they developed because they seemed right at particular times and in particular circumstances. By understanding what those circumstances were we can appreciate why the doctrines took the form they did, and what their strengths and weaknesses are.

The background

In the early Church, Christians were aware that Scripture included many texts that seemed irrelevant, incomprehensible, or morally objectionable. They talked about the New Testament, as well the Old, as "inspired", or "the word of God", but the way they treated them was quite different from the way Christians treat them now. They were rarely interested in historial accuracy. Characteristically they looked for deeper spiritual truths underlying the literal statements, and found them through processes like allegory or typology. Thus arose traditions of interpretation: on first reading a text may seem incredible or incomprehensible, but the tradition provided ways to make sense of it. In order to understand the Bible, then, one needed to take part in the tradition of interpretation which the Church offered. At this stage tradition and reason co-operated in the search for truth. Later they diverged. From the 11th century onwards, scientists were producing theories which contradicted Biblical texts. This led to the "faith and reason" debate in the universities. The synthesists, like Aquinas, tried to hold the two together in a single account of how we know things; but in the 14th century the debate was resolved into a dualistic system, best expressed by William of Ockham. To Ockham reason was to be used for the study of the physical, observable world; but unobservable spiritual matters were the domain of the Church, whose doctrines were to be accepted without it.

Ockham emphasized that the two systems for knowing things were quite distinct; neither side has any right to encroach on the territory of the other. This meant that reason has no business to reflect on the Church's doctrines: they just have to be accepted as divine revelation, supreme over human reason in the spiritual realm. An implication of this view was a heightened sense of certainty in theological matters; to deny the appropriateness of reason is to insist that the doctrine is beyond question.

This provided the background for the Reformation. Because they objected to some of the Catholic Church's practices, the Reformers rejected the Church's authority. Some, including Socinus and Melanchthon, made room for reason, but the overwhelming majority agreed with Ockham in rejecting it. They therefore needed an alternative court of appeal. Thus the supreme authority of the Bible came to be of paramount importance to them: Scripture needed to transcend the authority of both Church and reason, owing nothing to either. Luther, Calvin and Zwingli all emphasized that humanity was fallen, and human reason was therefore flawed.

By denying the legitimacy of reason in matters of faith, the Reformers undermined their own right to use reason in arguing their case. In the 19th century Nietzsche would follow this position to its logical conclusion, in which one refuses to argue but only asserts. Some 19th-century religious movements would copy the idea, and more recently, postmodernists have done so too; but it is difficult to see how one can do so consistently without being utterly unconvincing: to be persuaded, people need reasons.

If the authority of the Bible was supreme, nobody had the authority to interpret it. To grant anybody the right to declare authoritative interpretations of texts would be to give that person greater authority than Scripture. The Reformers therefore developed the doctrine of perspicuity, which states that the Bible is clear and persuasive. Anybody who can read should be able to understand it. It is possible, they claimed, to establish the Bible's clear teaching on everything of importance, and they set about establishing it. Soon, of course, the idea had to be modified, as disagreements arose about the meanings of texts; but it lasted long enough to put its stamp on Reformation theology, and to set a precedent that was to be revived in the 19th century.

The Reformers also claimed that the Bible was omnicompetent. It was widely accepted that it contains everything necessary for salvation; the Puritans also expected it to legislate for all aspects of human life. Luther and other Reformers did not go so far; they believed the laws in the Bible could be divided into two types: the moral ones – which Christians are obliged to obey – and the cultic or civil ones, which are no longer binding. This is the view expressed in Article 7 of the 39 Articles. Although it is still common in some Protestant Churches, Biblical scholars point out that the Bible itself does not recognize any such distinction.

The theory of the Bible's omnicompetence continues to be defended in two contrasting ways. According to one account it governs all matters, including the six-day creation, Noah's flood and the rejection of evolution. To others, Scripture's omnicompetence relates to all matters of faith, but no more. This presents a dilemma common today among conservative Evangelicals: either they must believe, not just in the six-day creation, but in all other Biblical accounts of physical phenomena, regardless of the scientific evidence to the contrary, or they must treat the Christian faith as a self-contained system totally disconnected from, and irrelevant to, public knowledge.

The doctrine of omnicompetence implies that truth, at least in matters of faith, is fixed for all time. There is no possibility of new insights, and therefore no point in looking for them. A new theory must, by definition, be un-Biblical and therefore wrong.

The Reformers faced the need to justify the greater authority they were attributing to the Bible, and to do so without appealing to tradition or reason. Luther appealed to the Bible's contents, and considered some parts more authoritative than others. Most scholars understand Calvin to have taught a doctrine of verbal inspiration; he described the apostles as "the sworn and authentic amanuenses of the Holy Spirit", used words like "dictating", and considered all the books equally inspired. The Scriptures, he taught, impress themselves on the human heart through the witness of the Holy Spirit, a witness that applies to the Bible and to nothing else. We owe to the Bible the same reverence that we owe to God, since it has proceeded from him alone, and has nothing merely human mixed in with it. The Scriptures are self-authenticating; they "obtain among believers only when men regard them as having sprung from heaven, as if there the living words of God were heard." Similarly Zwingli thought of the text itself as sacred, with an authority of its own. Deep within each person, he believed, there is a hidden longing for God's saving Word, which the Holy Spirit can elicit.

Running through this reason-denying system was the claim to certainty. It was generally believed, by Catholics and Protestants alike, that no account of theological truth was adequate unless it produced certainty. By rejecting the doctrine of Purgatory, Protestants faced a stark alternative between two possible afterlives, heaven and hell. This naturally increased anxiety; faith as saving knowledge was in practice a major concern, and since the only certainty available was psychologically induced rather than rationally proven, an inner sense of feeling certain was encouraged. It was destined to have a major impact on subsequent Evengelicalism; it opened the door to an emotional type of religion that emphasizes the role of the individual's feeling of closeness to the Spirit, and encourages those who have it to imagine they also have an error-free understanding of the Christian faith.

It is easy to understand the motivation of the Reformers for generating these doctrines. However, it remained the case, as patristic and medieval scholars had known, that such claims for Scripture cannot be reconciled with the text of the Bible itself. The discrepancy soon generated disagreements between Protestants about biblical interpretation, a problem accentuated by the doctrine that the meaning of all texts is perfectly clear. The result was a wide range of competing Protestant institutions claiming to be the supreme authority on matters of faith, claiming to accept pure divine revelation unalloyed by mere human reason.

In other circumstances it might have been possible to resolve many of the disagreements with the use of reasoned discussion. Because they rejected this process, it was not. The result was the bitter sectarianism, which still characterizes parts of Protestantism today where, as each sect struggles to stop true believers being attracted to competing doctrines, its leaders teach members exactly what to believe, warn them that doubts and questions are of the devil, give them strict rules for conversations with non-members, and encourage them in a conviction of certainty which provides a cheap sense of superiority and dispenses with the need to study the issues seriously.

The Anglican appeal to a balance between Scripture, reason and tradition, stemming from Richard Hooker, provides a sharp contrast. Hooker was less influenced by Ockham, more by Aquinas and the medieval synthesists. There is currently a debate about what he believed, because often his writing is obscure; the most likely explanation is that over time he became more sympathetic to the use of reason, but had to be careful what he said because, as a clergyman, he could not afford to contradict any of the 39 Articles.

Hooker accepted that Scripture teaches clearly whatever is necessary for salvation, but on secondary and indifferent matters, *adiaphora*, he argued that we have the light of reason and experience to guide us. Thirdly, we also have the authority of tradition. He denied that we could have absolute certainty: we only have "probable persuasions".

He saw that the Bible could not be self-authenticating. To accept the Bible's authority because the Bible claims it is what we today would call a circular argument; only if we already accept its authority in the first place does the conclusion follow. In accepting the Bible's authority, therefore, we have nothing else to guide us but reason and conscience. This means that the claim that the Bible contains the word of God is a proper subject for reasoned argument. "The authority of man is, if we mark it, the key which opens the door of entrance into the knowledge of the Scripture", for "Scripture could not teach us the things that are of God, unless we did credit men who have taught us that the words of Scripture do signify these things."

This view enabled Hooker to accept the legitimacy of change. Except in fundamental "articles concerning doctrine", change was a reality for the Church, which "has authority to establish that for an order at one time, which at another it may abolish, and in both do well."

Hooker's successors established the Anglican tradition that affirmed the authority of Scripture, reason and tradition, and settled for probability at the expense of certainty. By the end of the 17th century this position was the standard view of Anglicans across the theological spectrum, the main variation being that High Church Anglicans placed tradition above reason. If Anglicanism can be said to have developed a distinctive theology of its own, this is it. It is this tradition that is now under threat.

As the Enlightenment progressed, the claims for reason grew stronger. The Enlightenment's characteristic approach was motivated by a reaction against religious claims to authority. The Reformation and Counter-Reformation, with their anxieties about what we need to know for salvation, their claims to absolute certainty, and their willingness to fight one war after another in the interests of religious truth as they saw it, were perceived as a tragic era. What was needed was to learn how to live together in peace. This meant abandoning doctrines based on irreconcilable authoritarian traditions, and turning instead to shared public reason, where the evidence for any belief could be made publicly available, to be assessed by other people. The new and more scientific age was therefore expected to dispense with tradition; it expected all truths to be in principle discoverable through the use of reason by any individual. Enlightenment thinkers often therefore had very little historical sense. In effect, there was a swing of the pendulum from one extreme to the other; reason, instead of having no part to play, was considered capable of establishing all truths, for any individual who wanted to know, by starting from first principles and working everything out. In the 18th century some of the Deists argued that all the truths of Christianity could be established by reason, and raised the question whether revelation through Scripture was strictly necessary. The result was a simplified version of belief appealing to a small number of doctrines considered to be self-evident.

For Hooker, "reason" was a general term for thought processes that could work out what the truth might be, as opposed to accepting an authority without question The Enlightenment philosophers analyzed it; its central notion was rational deduction, as applied in mathematics and logic. Descartes' rationalist system was based on rational deduction from first principles: from his first principle, "I think, therefore I am", he deduced that he exists, then that God exists, and then that the external world exists.

Descartes' system of rationality is *foundationalist*: it begins with self-evident truths which cannot be doubted, and from which other truths can be deduced with certainty. Foundationalism was the dominant model for discovering truths throughout the Enlightenment. 20th-century theories have tended to prefer *coherentist* accounts. Coherentism argues that in practice we begin, not with first principles, but with where we are, with what we experience and think we know. As our experience grows, we make connections with other observations, and the things we think we know fit together in an ever-expanding web. Any part of the web may be wrong, but the more the parts cohere together in a consistent pattern, the more they support each other. Unlike foundationalism, coherentism never expects certainty.

The other main element of Enlightenment reason is *empiricism*:

we learn about the external world from our five senses. Locke developed a model of the mind, explaining how sense impressions get to it from the outside world; but we know that we dream and make mistakes, so it is harder to claim certainty on the basis of empiricism.

It became clear that much of what we think we know cannot be justified either rationally or empirically: the existence of God, causation, ethical norms, statements about the past, and other people's minds. One response, popular from the 1920s to the 1960s, was logical positivism, which insisted that rationalism and empiricism are the only means by which we can know anything, and argued that statements which cannot be verified in either of these ways must be meaningless. This made all religious language meaningless.

Here lies the weakness of the characteristic Enlightenment account of reason. Beginning with the assumption that all truth is open to discovery by the individual through empirical observation and rational deduction, it has been prone to deny the existence of anything which cannot be so established.

Since the 19th century there has been greater awareness of the importance of traditions of enquiry building up over the generations. Religious thought reflected it: the Oxford Movement, for example re-emphasized the role of tradition, and Newman produced a theory of the development of doctrine. The non-rational elements of religion were emphasized: personal religious experience, the emotions, intuition. In some ways this was a necessary corrective, but it also permitted the rise of a counter-cultural anti-intellectualism which reaffirmed Reformation doctrines. As these doctrines were reaffirmed, however, they were changed. The Reformers often developed doctrines and later changed their minds; the 19th century revivals of the doctrines often treated them, like Biblical texts, as true beyond question.

The debates over evolution and Biblical scholarship sharpened party lines. Some were willing to allow that the world was much older than previously thought, and that the gospels did not present a consistent account of the teaching of Jesus. Others insisted on the supremacy of the Bible over human reason, and rejected these new findings. A third response was the dualist view, leaving the physical world to science while reinterpreting the Bible and the Christian tradition in purely spiritual terms.

Currently all three approaches are very much with us. The theory of the authority of the Bible on all matters has developed an anti-evolutionist tradition, which is still influential. The dualist approach has, in practice, guided the development of most church institutions, as they carve out a role for themselves in a predominantly secular society. The reason-affirming tradition, with its stronger commitment to engaging with its host society, is still popular, but it generally represents those who have wider interests and are less likely to be influential in the Churches. It last achieved widespread popularity in the 1960s, an unfortunate time. Its affirmation of reason coincided with a time when Marxism and logical positivism were popular, both of which denied the existence of God. In addition it was commonly believed that science had disproved religion. "Liberal theology" came to be associated with "the death of God". It is hardly surprising that the 1970s saw a reaction against this version of liberalism.

Two theological traditions

Today the different positions have polarized into two mutually exclusive theological systems, each with its own account of how Churches should operate. These are usually referred to as "conservative" and "liberal". Neither of these words is an accurate description, but in the absence of generally accepted alternatives I shall use them. The beliefs of both conservatives and liberals vary widely; it would be foolish to claim that any one view is held by all conservatives or all liberals. Nevertheless, behind these two traditions lie two mutually exclusive *systems*, each with its own theology and ecclesiology. What, then, are their distinctive features?

The conservative methodology appeals to the supreme authority of the Bible within a foundationalist system: the Bible, perceived as a unitary entity, is the foundation from which all religious truths can be derived. Denying that either reason or tradition have authority to interpret the Bible, it has no use for public debate or research. This gives the tradition is *individualistic* feel: truth can be derived by any individual.

The theology deriving from this system is *closed* in two senses. Firstly, it does not – in theory – allow insights from non-Biblical sources. Statistics about the numbers of homosexuals, or psychological research into homosexual orientation are considered irrelevant to the ethics of the matter, as the Bible has spoken. Thus the tradition turns its back on its host society, in postmodern manner preferring to pay attention only to its own world: it is *inward looking*. Secondly, it denies the possibility of new insights developing in the future, since all true insights are already contained in the Bible. There is nothing new to discover. It is *backward looking*.

In practice, the conservative view accumulates doctrines. To take an example, the early Church spent immeasurable effort debating the person of Christ and the Trinity. Once the Councils of Nicæa and Chalcedon had decreed a particular position as normative, Arianism ceased to be one common view among others, and became instead an unacceptable view; to call someone an Arian became an accusation. Changes of this type are popular with the conservative tradition, as they invite Christians to consider the defeated view as definitely rejected for all time. In practice, therefore, conservatives appeal to authorities other than the Bible. Within Anglicanism the 39 Articles are a favorite, and even *Issues in Human Sexuality* seems recently to have been emerging from a discussion document into an authoritative statement of what all Anglicans must believe.

Foundationalist systems characteristically expect to deliver *certainty*, and this feature is still popular with the conservative tradition today. If one's own beliefs are certain to be true, it follows that people with conflicting beliefs are certain to be wrong. There is no sense in which they may just turn out to be right, or that anything is to be learned from them.

In practice, conservative views vary widely: it is certainly not the case that all conservatives agree with this summary. Nevertheless this system, with its own coherent logic and its distinctive theology, is the well-spring feeding the conservative lobby in the current debate. It is this system which grants them permission to repeat over and over again that by opposing homosexuality they are upholding the Bible's authority, while refusing to acknowledge alternative interpretations of the Bible presented by others. Without this system, the current opposition to gay bishops would not have an intellectual base.

By contrast, the characteristic liberal appeal is to the Anglican tradition which attributes authority to a balance of Scripture, reason and tradition. In practice Anglicans have not always achieved a satisfactory balance. The authority of each has been underrated at one time and overrated at another. In principle, though, it is recognized that each source of authority is prone to error if it is not checked by the others. The checking process is not reducible to an authoritative set of rules; it can only be done through reflection, using insights from whatever sources are available. This reflection is not the preserve of any individual; different people provide different insights. Those who are committed to the balance of Scripture, reason and tradition must therefore also be committed to public debate, research and reflection.

By recognizing more than one authority, none of which is inerrant, this tradition is *coherentist* rather than foundationalist. It expects to live with uncertainty, learning piecemeal, always allowing for the possibility that each of its valued doctrines may at some stage be modified or rejected.

Whereas the appeal to Scripture alone characteristically generates an individualistic approach to religious commitment – and the appeal to tradition alone is characteristically communitarian – the appeal to a balance of authorities maintained by open public reflection affirms the roles of both individual and community, informing each other. It is *interrelational*.

Because liberalism believes that we may learn from anybody at all, it expects us to listen to those from other traditions. It is *respectful*.

As a theological system it is *open*. By denying that religion lives in a world of its own, and expecting religious insights to inform, and in turn be informed by, insights from outside the world of religion, it expects to be *engaged* in matters which concern its host society and therefore *outward looking*. Similarly, its coherentist approach allows for the possibility that new insights may arise which are not deducible from inherited authorities, but are nevertheless true. This allows the search for religious truth to be *forward looking* and therefore *creative*. As the Lambeth 1988 Conference Report puts it:

> Tradition and reason, then, are two distinct contexts in which the Scriptures speak and out of which they are interpreted. It is in the interplay and the conflict between them – between

the common mind of the Church and the common mind of a culture – that the meaning of the Gospel for a particular time and place is to be discerned. Indeed it could be argued that tradition – what we have called the 'mind' of the Church – is the repository of just such discernments stimulated by the tradition and the language of a particular culture. To be involved in this dialogical situation is always uncomfortable. It becomes dangerous, perhaps, only when what is properly a dialogue becomes a monologue delivered at length by only one of its parties. Tradition and reason need each other if God's Word is to be shared.

Two accounts of the Church

These divergent theological traditions generate equally divergent expectations about how Churches should operate. Again, opinions vary widely, but behind them lie two mutually exclusive ecclesiologies. For conservative Churches, with their foundationalist approach, the truths to be learned have all been established in the past. Knowledge is uni-directional, from those who have already acquired it to those still learning. There is no role for creativity: a new answer must be a wrong answer. The group discussion is not a potential source of new truths, only a means for learning old ones.

The most appropriate structure is therefore hierarchical. At the top is the person with the greatest teaching authority. The gathered Church is where doctrine is transmitted. Given the strong sense of certainty, there is limited room for differences of opinion. Whereas such a church may welcome attenders with contrasting beliefs, positions of leadership need to be restricted to those who accept the Church's teaching on all matters considered important. To grant a leadership post to a dissident would dilute the sense of certainty with which doctrines are taught, and therefore undermine the very purpose of the Church. To invite church members to hear both sides of a disagreement and make up their own minds would be to exalt reason above Scripture.

Conservative Churches emphasize their distinctiveness: the doctrines they teach most strongly are those, which separate them from their host societies. Opposition to alcohol, abortion and homosexuality have all served their turn. As well as providing teaching, church services revitalize allegiance and the sense of being different from non-members. It is important that members agree with each other and disagree with outsiders. Conservatives therefore are unwilling to accept that the true Christian community is divided over ethical issues like gay bishops; they prefer to describe it as a division between the true Christian community on the one hand and outsiders on the other. Part of their response to the debate is, therefore, to redefine the true Church so as to exclude those with whom they disagree.

For these reasons conservatives find it unacceptable for the Anglican Communion to acknowledge Gene Robinson's status as a bishop. The Church's view on homosexuality has been established once and for all, and cannot be changed. For a person who rejects it to be appointed to a bishopric undermines the whole Church, since a central function of churches and their bishops is to provide worshippers with truths which are beyond question. Conservatives, therefore, argue that they cannot tolerate the appointment to a bishopric of someone who publicly rejects accepted doctrine.

What is revealed is an intolerance, which demands exclusion. In effect it claims for conservatives the right to veto episcopal appointments. Within Anglicanism it is a new development: until now Protestants and Catholics alike have accepted that Anglicanism includes bishops with whom they disagree. Though new to Anglicanism, however, it is familiar to the conservative theological tradition. Since the early days of the Reformation, many Churches have claimed for themselves the true doctrines of uninterpreted revelation, and the rejection of reason has prevented reconciliation between competing theories. The history of sectarian Calvinism has liberally shown how the conviction of absolute certainty generates intolerance of those who disagree, and a willingness to exlude them. The result is a tendency to split into competing sects.

It is all the more strange that religion should be the carrier of this certainty-based sectarianism, since throughout history one of the central ethical claims of all the world's major religions has been that each of us needs to recognize other people as equally human, equally deserving of respect, as ourselves.

The "problem of other minds" is a well established theme in philosophy, but even more well established is the need to accept the reality of other people's minds – with their feelings and beliefs – as equally real, and deserving of respect, as our own. Yet here in this post-Ockhamite religious tradition there exists a well established doctrine that our own minds, and the minds of our chosen sect, access truth with a reliability and certainty which is not available to other people.

In all other fields of discourse this would be recognized as pure bigotry. When Ockham published his dualist system, he took it for granted that there was only one authority on spiritual matters. When Descartes published his rationalist theory designed to deduce certainties from first principles, he could assume that, if he was right, a consensus would develop round it. Since the Reformation, competing institutions have been claiming to know the truth with certainty, and have disagreed with each other about what that truth is. Major public debates have also characterized other fields of discourse – sub-atomic physics, astronomy, biology, psychology and economics, to name a few recent ones – and yet in all these debates the recognized procedure has been for both sides to put their theories, and the evidence for them, in the public realm, where those with the skills can examine the strength of the arguments and work towards consensus. Only in the case of religion has a reason-denying tradition been so well established that it can effectively prevent any such resolution of disagreement. Western Europe and North America have long grown used to large numbers of Churches led by people who confidently proclaim doctrines which they think they know with certainty, fully aware that down the street another church leader proclaims conflicting truths with an equal sense of certainty. We have all grown used to this absurdity, used to the fact that behaviour which is unacceptable everywhere else is normal in the world of religion. Since anybody else who operated like this would be condemned for bigotry, it is difficult to see why religious leaders should be exempt.

Again, of course, most conservatives do not agree with everything in this position. Nevertheless it is this view which provides the intellectual framework upon which the current campaign against gay bishops is being conducted. It is this view which provides the ecclesiology which cannot tolerate them. Without the active campaigning for this ecclesiology, it would have been clear to all that the Anglican approach to the structure of churches and their means of decision-making can comfortably tolerate gay bishops while a public debate about them proceeds.

For liberals there is no single source of truth, no simple system of deduction, no absolute certainty. The search for truth takes place within the community, and proceeds not by simply transmitting information from teachers to learners, but by seeking information from as wide a variety of sources as possible.

To the extent that this takes place within the church, the ideal structure is a democratic one. Everybody has something to learn and something to contribute. A "pure" church of the carefully selected, all agreeing with each other, would be a dull church, offering nothing new. Instead, the church needs to hear divergent voices. It is therefore better for it to be inclusive, so that different views can be heard with respect, considered and debated. Truth emerges not by putting up barriers against error but by knocking them down. Church discussion groups can be genuinely creative, encouraged to make new discoveries. Similarly, if church leaders disagree with each other on significant issues, there is a shared understanding of reasoned discourse upon which public debate can proceed.

For liberals, what goes on in church is only part of the picture. Outsiders also have much to teach us. This is the case both because divine revelation is not confined to any one source, and also because religious understanding, far from being hermetically sealed from other forms of knowledge, engages with them, expecting to contribute to them and to learn from them. The distinction between members and non-members of a church is therefore less important and can afford to be fuzzier. The church at its best is *inclusive*.

The price to pay is lack of certainty. We can never be absolutely sure that our beliefs are true, as only God is infallible. Of course the opinions we hold are the ones we believe to be true, but we may be wrong. Openness and humility are appropriate to faith, as to all else. At the same time, as we think our search for truth is important, we carry on exploring and arguing, expecting truth to emerge through public debate.

For liberals, therefore, the debate about gay bishops can take place *within* the Church, allowing both sides to be heard. This has, in practice, been the way Anglicanism has dealt with disagreements since the 17th century. Anglicans have been strongly divided over a great many issues, among them slavery, evolution, biblical criticism, women in the ordained ministry, remarriage after divorce, capital punishment and contraception. In every one of these issues the opponents of change had the lion's share of the Biblical texts; nevertheless, in every case the majority Anglican view has changed. The change took time. The time was made available because the Church permitted its bishops, clergy and laity to express views at variance with the inherited position. Alternative episcopal oversight was not considered necessary, even by the opponents of slavery in the dioceses of slave-owning bishops.

Summary

Anglicanism today, therefore, contains within it two contrasting theological traditions, each with its own account of how churches should organize themselves and make decisions. The two are so different that no organization can be governed in both ways at once. There cannot be a genuine debate between people who believe in genuine debate and people who do not. There cannot be compromise between those who are willing to compromise and those who are not. We have to choose.

The tradition which has heretofore characterized Anglicanism has been open and inclusive. It has not expected certainty in doctrine, and has therefore been prepared to tolerate differences of opinion and open debate, leading sometimes to changes in its doctrinal and ethical views.

Characteristically, Anglican inclusiveness has had a laid back, "open house" approach. Over the last forty years church leaders, anxious about declining numbers, have been only too keen to encourage clergy who are good at building up large congregations. At first they turned a blind eye to the fact that they were ordaining people whose spiritual home was in authoritarian sectarianism rather than Anglicanism; or perhaps they thought that there should be room in a broad church for them too. At first they were a small minority respecting the fact that their views did not represent the Church as a whole. Now they have gained sufficient influence to challenge the decision-making procedures of the Anglican Communion as a whole.

The campaign raises that question which dogs all liberal theory: if we believe in inclusiveness, do we include the excluders?

Our inclusiveness needs to be protected if it is to survive. We cannot continue to feed the hand that bites us. We therefore need to do the opposite of what we normally do. We need, ironically, to set limits to acceptable belief, not on homosexuality – which is just one ethical issue among many – but on how the Church makes decisions. To retain our inclusiveness we now need, formally, to reject as incompatible with Anglicanism, the view that Churches should be exclusive.

Many conservatives are campaigning for the Anglican Communion to discipline Bishop Robinson and those who support him. If my argument is accepted, they are the ones who should be disciplined for undermining the Church's traditional procedures and methods of decision-making. It would have been better if the Windsor Report had told them that if they are determined to maintain their policy of excluding those who disagree, their true home is in the authoritarian sects. If they want to be Anglicans, they must accept the inclusive character of Anglicanism.

It seems absurd to say that in the interests of inclusiveness we need to do some excluding. Yet this is the nature of openness and freedom: because they are open to abuse, they are easily undermined. If we are to retain our tradition, we can no longer take it for granted. We need to protect it.

Jonathan Clatworthy is General Secretary of the Modern Churchpeople's Union.

CONCLUSION

Jonathan Clatworthy

The Windsor Report has announced its recommendations and explained its reasons. At the time of writing it is up to the various parts of the Anglican Communion to decide what to make of it. From a liberal point of view it is inviting the Church to move in the wrong direction. This book has described the reasons: it seeks to make Anglicanism more centralized and authoritarian, less tolerant and diverse. It takes for granted that homosexuality is morally wrong and that the actions of New Westminster and New Hampshire were out of order.

It begins by emphasizing the importance of unity. What it means by unity, we gradually discover, is uniformity out of character with the past history of the church. In practice unity is best maintained when diversity of belief and practice is permitted; when it is not, those who disagree have no option but to separate. The only satisfactory solution to the present disagreement, we believe, is for those who oppose homosexuality to accept that other Christians, equally committed to their faith and equally theologically informed, have a different view and have just as much right to be Anglicans. Those who refuse to accept this diversity of views must face the fact that their views on diversity and inclusiveness are at odds with Anglicanism; if they are determined to impose their views on others, they should do so outside Anglicanism.

In the interests of centralization the Report proposes an increase in the powers of the Archbishop of Canterbury and the introduction of a "Communion law" and a "common Anglican covenant" as communion-wide authorities. The purpose of these changes is to reduce the freedoms of provinces and bishops in order to prevent a repetition of the innovations that took place at New Westminster and New Hampshire. Liberals believe this would be a major step in the wrong direction. The history of most institutions, including the Church, shows that the best methods for developing successful innovations are from bottom upwards, not top downwards.

An additional problem is that the proposals are so restrictive that it would be very difficult for any innovations to be introduced at all; in effect the Anglican Communion would become static, stuck in a time warp. This can be seen from its discussion of *adiaphora*, matters which are not essential to the Communion as a whole and can therefore be decided by the provinces for themselves. Questions concerning the whole Communion, it decrees, need to involve the whole Communion in their decision-making. This sounds fine: but it has nothing to do with the present debate, as Gene Robinson is Bishop only of New Hampshire and the same-sex blessing rite is available only in New Westminster.

The Report gets round this problem by excluding from the category of *adiaphora* any matters which "a sufficient number of other Christians will find scandalous and offensive, either in the sense that they will be led into acting against their own consciences or that they will be forced, for conscience' sake, to break fellowship with those who go ahead". This criterion has not previously been part of Anglican ecclesiology. To liberals it looks as though it has been framed precisely in order to justify rejecting the same-sex blessings and Robinson's consecration. As a working principle it is clearly unsatisfactory. Christians vary widely in their judgments of what would count as scandalous or offensive. Many bishops – probably most – engage in at least one activity which is considered scandalous or offensive by some people somewhere in the worldwide Anglican Communion, whether it be drinking alcohol, supporting the armed forces, supporting or opposing abortion, or engaging in usury by holding an account in a building society. If this criterion is formally incorporated into Anglican decision making, liberals will have little or no use for it, as they prefer the Church to be inclusive. Its primary – probably its only – use will be by intolerant minorities determined to impose their views on the Church as a whole.

The "sufficient number" would need to be precisely defined. Once defined, it would set a target for the petition signing of campaigning organizations. Any organization which achieved the figure would then be in a position to veto any change, or the appointment of any bishop, provided only that they claimed it offended their consciences. Gentle souls may, perhaps, feel that no self-respecting Christian organization would stoop so low as to be so unscrupulous. Liberals reply that this is precisely what is happening now.

To discuss the ethics of homosexuality was outside the Report's remit, but it worked on the basis that the Anglican Communion considers homosexuality immoral. The main reasons given are the Biblical condemnations and 1998 Lambeth Conference resolution.

Liberals question both these reasons. People who oppose homosexuality on the basis of Scripture are invariably selective in their use of it. There are over six hundred commands in the Bible, the majority of which are ignored by Christians today. Lambeth Conference resolutions are not binding. The 1998 resolution in particular is hedged with question marks, as an unusually large number of African bishops attended that conference, and there have been suspicions – not denied, let alone refuted – that some of them were paid to attend, with the specific purpose of voting in favor of it. If it had been an Act of Parliament, at the very least it would have been challenged in the courts.

It is on these dubious bases that the Report judges the dioceses of New Westminster and New Hampshire to have been at fault. It does not ask them to repent, but it does ask them to regret their actions. In fact, those responsible for the innovations did nothing wrong, either morally or constitutionally. In effect the Report is proposing to change the rules of the Anglican Communion and apply the new rules retrospectively to these actions. Retrospectively applied legislation would certainly contravene accepted constitutional procedures. If the Communion does decide to make the 1998 Lambeth Conference resolution binding on all Anglicans, and expect those who supported Robinson's consecration to withdraw from their representative functions, the matter will not rest there. Inevitably the question will arise about the seventy bishops who voted against it. It will seem only proper that they, too, should be invited to regret their action and withdraw from representative functions.

The Report shows great sympathy for the pain, which the actions in New Westminster and New Hampshire caused to those who oppose homosexuality – and not a word concerning the pain caused to homosexuals themselves. This is an astonishing reversal of any credible moral position. If, for example, it showed sympathy for the pain caused to white supremacists, who believed that blacks should be slaves but who were forced by law to treat blacks as equals, it would be clear to all that the pain caused to the white supremacists does not have the same moral right to sympathy as the pain caused to black slaves. Similarly, the pain caused to homosexuals by the current discrimination affects their whole lives and is inescapable; the pain caused to the opponents of homosexuality when a homosexual becomes a bishop is a self-inflicted pain based on a choice to hold, and feel strongly about, a particular opinion. As Gill Cooke says, it is a basic rule in first aid that, when dealing with more than one casualty, one should focus on the silent ones first, as they are usually suffering more than the ones making most noise. So it is in this case. The ones making most noise do not suffer discrimination in education and jobs. They do not get beaten up on the street just for being what they are.

The Report presents opposition to homosexuality as the view of the overwhelming majority of Anglicans. Liberals doubt this. Much depends on how we count. What we have witnessed is a highly organized campaign, run by a small number of people and claiming the support of large numbers. Of those large numbers, most simply attend a church or belong to a diocese, which has an official policy of opposing homosexuality. The individuals being counted may not have a view on the issue, or may even be homosexuals themselves. Indeed, although most of the poorer countries have public ethical norms, which oppose homosexuality, they also have homosexuals, and many priests among them.

The nature of that campaign is itself worthy of comment. Clergy and parishes have threatened to refuse to recognize their diocesan bishop simply on the ground that the bishop supports Gene Robinson's consecration. Parishes have threatened to withdraw their giving if they do not get their way. Threats have been issued to Robinson's life. While declining to comment on these threats, Windsor does note that some bishops have intervened in other provinces to offer "alternative episcopal oversight". It asks them to express regret and cease intervening, while sympathizing with the fact that they felt a conscientious duty to do so. However there is no suggestion that they should not be invited to future Communion-wide events. Nor is there a similar sympathy for ECUSA's sense of conscientious duty. That failure to notice that the innovators conscientiously believe they did the right thing, is a major weakness. It runs through the whole Report, vitiating its attempts to be even-handed.

To summarize, the issues might be described under three headings. Firstly, the authors of this book disagree with the Report's proposal to give the Anglican Communion a more centralized and hierarchical power structure. In our view, God's revelation is not restricted to archbishops and international committees. Secondly, we believe in accepting diversity of belief and practice. The greater uniformity being sought by the Report will, contrary to its intentions, foster greater disunity as people discover that their own views are no longer considered acceptable. Thirdly, the Report works on the basis that the Anglican Communion has reached a consensus that homosexuality is immoral. If this had been the case, there would have been no remaining controversy, and the Archbishop would not asked the Commission to produce this Report.

Recently published by O Books

The Anglican Quilt
Robert Van de Weyer

This book offers a detailed plan for resolving the present crisis over homosexuality in the Anglican Church, prompted by the appointment of openly gay bishops in the USA and England, and the blessing of a gay partnership in Canada.

Racing the roots of the crisis back to the foundations of Anglicanism over four centuries ago, Robert Van de Weyer shows why ancient divisions have grown wider in recent decades. He argues that the two sides now need separate Episcopal arrangements – yet both sides have much to gain by remaining together in a single body.

A very important contribution.
George Carey, former Archbishop of Canterbury

There is much in it to admire…I have no alternative to offer.
John Habgood, former Archbishop of York

It should be read by everybody who cares about the future of the Anglican Church.
Nicholas Stacey, Clergyman and former deputy director of Oxfam

The author offers solutions that are far preferable to schism and strife.
William Frend, retired Professor of Ecclesiastical History at Glasgow University.

I find it both persuasive and stimulating.
Anthony Howard, Times columnist and commentator of Church of England affairs

Stimulating, controversial, and full of good sense.
Jack Nicholls, Bishop of Sheffield

Robert Van de Weyer is a priest in the Church of England and has ministered in a small village near Cambridge since 1982. He has written over fifty books on theology, world religions, philosophy, church history and economics.